What We Can REALLY Learn from the Rich and Famous

*Publication of this book was made possible through
the generosity of my dear friend and congregant
MARVIN H. WEINER.*

What We Can REALLY Learn from the Rich and Famous

*A Selection of Ponderings,
Contemplations, and Inspirations*

By

Rabbi Mitchell Wohlberg

ISBN: 978-0-578-25279-7 (paperback)

To Sherry

"A great marriage is not when the "perfect couple" comes together. It is when an imperfect couple learns to enjoy their differences."

—Dave Meurer

CONTENTS

INTRODUCTION

Everybody does have a book in them ... but in most cases that's where it should stay!
                                    —Christopher Hitchens

Christopher Hitchens had a keen mind. I *hope* he was not thinking of this book when he wrote those words!

As a rabbi of Baltimore's Beth Tfiloh Congregation for more than forty years, I have been called upon to deliver some two thousand sermons, trying to connect biblical events with contemporary issues. My subject matters have ranged from Adam to Trump, Eve to Lady Gaga, and all points in between. As diverse as the subjects may have been, in looking back, I cannot help but note that most sermons contained at least one quote (and sometimes several) from someone else. I guess I must have thought all those philosophers, actors, athletes, writers, singers, and politicians whom I quoted were expressing key ideas and important insights better than I could have. To help make sermons topical, almost invariably my quotes came from the "rich and famous."

The phrase *rich and famous* is so popular that it has been used as a title of a movie, play, show, and song. I, like most others, invariably turn to the "rich and famous" because they are rich and famous, and most everyone, deep down inside, wishes they could emulate them. Bill Murray once said (here I go quoting one of them again), "I always like to say to people who want to be rich and famous, try being rich first. See if that doesn't cover most of it. There's not much downside about being rich other than paying taxes and having your relatives ask you for money. But when you become famous, you end up with a twenty-four-hour-job."[1]

Yes, when you become famous, everyone is watching you, following you, listening to you, and learning from you … even a rabbi and his congregation in Baltimore!

The truth of the matter is this selection from my two thousand sermons and the quotes they contain would never have made it into this book if not for the fact that I have been blessed with a warm, encouraging, even applauding congregation who took my words to heart. The age of Zoom has shown us that no matter how good a speaker or entertainer looks on Zoom, there is nothing like having a live audience! That explains why all professional sports shown on television during the coronavirus pandemic had profound rates of attrition. The game just wasn't the same without the fans! It was my congregational "fans" who inspired and uplifted me and made this book possible, along with a major helping hand from my longtime administrative assistant, Arlene Abramson, and the folks at Elite Authors.

So let's get to the words of the rich and famous and learn from them what to do—and often what not to do!

Mitchell Wohlberg

Remember what Frank Rich wrote: "In a country where there is no royalty and where, post-Watergate, politicians are held in almost universal contempt, celebrity is next to Godliness. Indeed, we want to believe in celebrities for the same reason we want to believe in God: their omnipotence and invincibility, however illusory, hold out the promise that we, too, have a crack at immortality."[2]

Hopeful Thoughts
for Modern Times

STARGAZING

I want all those kids to do what I do, to look up to me. I want all the kids to copulate me.

—Andre Dawson

Andre Dawson, nicknamed Awesome Dawson, was a 2010 inductee into the National Baseball Hall of Fame. No wonder he wanted kids to "copulate" him! And they did. Hero worship of an athlete, in and of itself, can be beneficial. From them, we can learn the importance of practice, perseverance, "grit," and so on. But often, hero worship borders on idolatry. After the death of Diego Maradona at the start of 2021, soccer fans mourned throughout the world. But nowhere was the mourning more intense than in Argentina's Church of Maradona. Yes, the Church of Maradona has followers all over, from Brazil and Mexico to Spain, Italy, and beyond. The church has its own Ten Commandments, and the tenth commandment is this: "Name your first son Diego"—after the man they worship.[3]

Whom do you look up to? Whom do you wish to emulate? Whom do you seek out for guidance? In ancient times, people looked to the stars for direction. We moderns seem to do the same ... but we look to living stars.

In 2018, Taylor Swift had 112 million followers on Instagram—that's more than a hundred million followers anxious to hear whatever she had to say. Then Taylor Swift spoke ... and people listened! Before that year's election, Taylor Swift endorsed two candidates in her native Tennessee for the first time. She told her followers to register and vote. According to Vote.org, sixty-five thousand registrations came in within twenty-four hours![4] The voter site within those same twenty-four hours had 155,940 unique visitors, compared to the usual average of fourteen thousand. As the spokesperson for Vote.org put it, "Thank God for Taylor Swift!"

And Taylor Swift ranked only ninth in popularity on Instagram. Do you know who has even larger followings? Such distinguished people of letters as Selena Gomez, Ariana Grande, Kylie Jenner, and, of course, one of the great thinkers of our time: Kim Kardashian. What do they know?

What does Taylor Swift got that I ain't got? Why do people follow her advice when it comes to politics? Yes, there has always been "hero" worship. We have worshipped celebrities for their exceptional achievements in sports and in the arts. But to seek and heed their advice? To emulate them? To see audiences hanging on their every word? Journalist and author Peter Carlson once wrote, "In France, philosophers are celebrities. In the United States, celebrities are philosophers."[5] But why?

Every week *People* magazine publishes a story about the life of some celebrity, one of the rich and famous. And do you know what you learn if you read that story? That these people have their full share of problems, just like we not-so-rich-and-famous people do. One is going through a messy divorce, and one has checked herself into a rehab center for drug abuse. You read about failed relationships, alcoholism, talents squandered, and fortunes and families lost through narcissistic excess. These are people you would think have it all—unlimited wealth, incredible fame, sexual magnetism, the homes and the cars and the svelte bodies that we all dream about. We follow their every move on Facebook, Instagram, etc. And yet when you read about them in more detail, you find that they are living what Henry Thoreau once called "lives of quiet desperation."[6]

Do you know whose picture has appeared on the cover of *People* magazine more than anyone else's—for a grand total of fifty-five times? The late Diana, Princess of Wales. If you looked at her life from the outside, she had it all: a storybook royal wedding, a prince of a husband, enormous wealth, great beauty. Who would have believed that she was so miserably unhappy in that marriage that she fell victim to bulimia, is rumored to have made a suicide attempt, and was driven to extramarital affairs? *People* magazine, page by page, week after week, shows us how empty and lonely and desperate the lives of so many of the rich and famous really are, how much they are really missing. And these are the people we look up to?

In December 2020, Joseph Epstein wrote an op-ed in the *Wall Street Journal* ridiculing First Lady Jill Biden's title of *Dr.* and claiming *kiddo* would be more appropriate for a woman with a doctorate in education.[7] A few days later, Heidi Stevens wrote a scathing reply in the *Chicago Tribune*. In it, she quoted a former professor of hers, Lola Burnham, a journalism professor at Eastern Illinois University.

In America, we have this strange need to tear down people who have put in the effort to delve into and specialize in an academic field, to make themselves experts by their intense study. We celebrate athletes who rise to the top of their game. We celebrate actors who win awards. And we just love rich people whose only accomplishment was to inherit wealth … but as a society we seem to have nothing but scorn for people who make reading, observing, studying, experimenting, and, yes, thinking the focus of their professional lives. These days, a huge chunk of our society even scorns those with medical degrees and advanced degrees in the sciences.[8]

Al Gore got it right when he said, "The planet is in distress, and all of the attention is on Paris Hilton."[9]

We would do well to reflect on what Cassius says to Brutus in Shakespeare's *Julius Caesar.*

The fault, dear Brutus, is not in our stars,

But in ourselves, that we are underlings.

It is not fate that rules our lives; we don't always need to look up to those with fame and wealth as if their superior luck gives them greater wisdom. In the end, our faults and our fates alike are in our own hands.

Remember what Joe Theismann said: "Nobody in football should be called a genius. A genius is a guy like Norman Einstein."[10]

MONEY

The truth is that at this stage of life, I don't really need
the money. If you can't live on what I make in my present
contract, there's something wrong with you.

—Jay Leno

In March 2004, Jay Leno renegotiated his contract with NBC.
Every night, more than six million viewers tuned in to the
Tonight Show with Jay Leno, nearly two million more viewers than
David Letterman's show. In fact, 15 percent of NBC's profits
came from the *Tonight Show with Jay Leno*. Jay Leno had been
getting a "measly" $16 million a year, while David Letterman had
been getting $31 million a year. So after the announcement of his
new contract, the first question the reporters asked Leno was this:
How much of a raise did you get? Jay Leno's answer? He affirmed
that he got a raise but added, "I don't need the money. If you can't
live on what I make, there's something wrong with you."[11]

Two years earlier, David Letterman had threatened to leave CBS
because he was making $30 million a year. He was only getting paid
only $150,000 an hour! And he wasn't satisfied! So who was better off?

There's a famous anecdote about something novelist F. Scott
Fitzgerald supposedly once said to Ernest Hemingway.

"You know," said Fitzgerald, "the rich are different from you and me."

"Yes," Hemingway replied. "They've got more money."[12]

That's it!

There is a story about a US investment banker standing at the pier of a small coastal Mexican village when a small boat with just one fisherman docked. Inside the small boat were several large yellowfin tuna. The banker complimented the man on the quality of his fish and asked how long it took to catch them.

The fisherman replied, "Only a little while."

The banker then asked why didn't he stay out longer and catch more fish. The man said he had enough to support his family's immediate needs. The banker then asked the fisherman, "What do you do with the rest of your time?"

The Mexican fisherman said, "I sleep late; fish a little; play with my children; take siesta with my wife, Maria; and stroll into the village each evening, where I sip wine and play guitar with my amigos. I have a full and busy life, señor."

The banker scoffed. "I am a Harvard MBA and could help you. You should spend more time fishing and, with the proceeds, buy a bigger boat; with the proceeds from the bigger boat, you could buy several boats. Eventually you would have a fleet of fishing boats. Instead of selling your catch to a middleman, you would sell directly to the processor, eventually opening your own cannery. You would control the product, processing, and distribution. You would need to leave this small coastal fishing village and move to Mexico City, then Los Angeles, and eventually New York City, where you would run your expanding enterprise."

The Mexican fisherman asked, "But señor, how long will this all take?"

To which the banker replied, "Fifteen to twenty years."

"But what then, señor?"

The banker laughed and said, "That's the best part! When the time is right, you would announce an IPO and sell your company stock to the public and become very rich. You would make millions!"

"Millions, señor? Then what?"

The banker said, "Then you would retire. Move to a small coastal fishing village, take siesta with your wife, play with your kids, and stroll to the village in the evenings, where you would sip wine and play your guitar with your amigos!"

No wonder it is often said that no one on their deathbed expresses regret over not having spent more time at the office!

So I ask you, Do we really need to have as much as we think we do? Are the things for which we work so hard really all necessities? And if they are, then how is it that so many generations before us were able to get along without them?

After being caught cheating, cyclist Lance Armstrong wrote in a statement, "There comes a point in every man's life when he has to say, 'Enough is enough!'"[13] Armstrong realized he'd made the mistake of waiting too long to say it. If you are wise and if you are healthy, then when you reach that point, you realize it and behave accordingly. Jay Leno was able to say enough was enough. If you are never able to say those words, no matter what you earn or what you have, you will never be content.

In March 2000, there was an interview in the *New York Times* with a man named Nelson Peltz. After making it rich by investing in troubled companies in the 1980s, he had appeared on the Forbes list of the wealthiest executives for almost a decade. But listen to what he said in the interview: "I'm like old money these days. You see these young guys worth $3 billion to $4 billion, and you think to yourself, 'What have I done wrong?' I feel like the guy who has to say to his kids, 'Go back to work because we can't make ends meet anymore.'"[14]

"Go back to work." And for what?

"There is no rest for the weary," Jeff Bezos, the founder of Amazon, wrote in a 1998 shareholder letter. "I constantly remind our employees to be afraid, to wake up every morning terrified."[15] For that, the rich children of a rich father should "Go back to work"? Work is supposed to help provide us with rest and relaxation, the freedom to do what we want to do. And yet for all too many, our work ties us down!

In an interview with Paul Zimmerman, film critic for *Newsweek* magazine, playwright Neil Simon once said, "Money brings some happiness. But after a certain point, it just brings more money."

Remember what the Beatles sang: "1 don't care too much for money; money can't buy me love."

REPEAT OFFENDERS

> When you make a mistake, there are only three things you should ever do about it: admit it, learn from it, and don't repeat it.
>
> —Paul "Bear" Bryant

We all make mistakes! A Weight Watchers booklet once contained the following errata notice: "The recipe for the Bacon and Egg Breakfast Tower on page six of *KickStart Your Cooking* serves twelve people, not one."

Yes, we all make mistakes, but do we learn from them?

Albert Einstein, considered the greatest mind of the twentieth century, is supposed to have come up with a definition of insanity that has become immortalized: "Insanity is doing the same thing over and over and expecting different results."[16] In golf, you are given a mulligan (a do-over after a first attempt has gone completely awry) in the hope and expectation that you won't repeat the same mistake.

Let me ask you a question: What do a past US president, several might-have-been presidents, a few governors, a World Bank director, a former Dutch prime minister, an Israeli ex-president, and one of the greatest golfers of our time all have in common?

I read an article about all of them on the CNN website. The article was about Bill Clinton, Governor Mark Sanford, Dominique Strauss-Kahn, Eliot Spitzer, Moshe Katsav, John Edwards, and Tiger Woods, and it was entitled "Are Men Stupid?"[17] I don't think men are stupid; I think they're insane!

Each of these men witnessed what happened to men who had, like him, previously held positions of power; each of them saw the downfall of those men for their infidelities and indiscretions, and then each one went and made the same mistake as all the previous men! Donald Trump would have been wise to take his own advice when he said, "Always try to learn from other people's mistakes, not your own—it is much cheaper that way!"

But it's not just the rich and famous, and it's not just the mistakes of others. This is a failing of so many of us who somehow don't learn from our own mistakes. What is the saying? "There is no fool like an old fool"? Yes, it is true, because when you're old, you shouldn't be a fool anymore. You shouldn't be making the same mistakes and doing the same things wrong. And yet I see it all the time! People never learn!

Most of the people who come to my office rarely come with a new problem. Whatever they're struggling with is not something that has happened for the first time. It's an old problem that they have allowed to fester and repeat, again and again and again. Tales of spousal infidelity, of abuse, of a friend's betrayal, of business partners cheating, of mistakes made with children, of people taking advantage … and I always quietly wonder, "Why did you wait so long? Why did you put up with this?"

The answer is always "Because I thought things would change" or "Because I thought I would get used to it" or "Because I thought it would stop."

Hope is important, but the reality is "Fool me once, shame on you. Fool me twice, shame on me!" Or as iconic Speaker of the House Sam Rayburn used to say, "There is no education in the second kick of a mule."[18] It's not easy for someone to let go of old problems because they're actually almost comforting. The devil you know is better than the devil you don't. However, people cling to old problems blindly, wondering why their lives don't change, don't improve. For things to change, they must have courage to encounter new problems and make new mistakes. Maybe we will never stop making mistakes, but maybe our job is to try to make new ones.

There is a popular Jim Carrey movie called *Liar Liar*, which has a few memorable lines, but one that always strikes me is the one where he asks, "Where would Tina Turner be right now if she rolled over and said, 'Hit me again, Ike.'"

For those not in the know, let me tell you a little something about Ike and Tina Turner. Tina Turner is one of the great rhythm and blues singers of our time, but she suffered through years of abuse from her husband, Ike Turner. Her career started with her marrying Ike and being the singer for his revue. He claimed that he made her everything she is. We don't know about that, but what we do know is that Ike's complete dominance over her life finally became too much for Tina, and after an unsuccessful suicide attempt, in 1975 she walked out on him with nothing more than thirty-six cents and a gas station credit card. On her own and starting from nothing, she rose to be one of the most dynamic and iconic entertainers of our time. That could not have happened had she, as Jim Carrey noted, rolled over and allowed Ike to keep hitting her.

Yes, there has to come a time when we learn from our mistakes and stop repeating them. All of us make mistakes, but none of us have to repeat them. Maimonides put it so well:

What constitutes true repentance? If the sinner has the opportunity of committing once again the sinful act, and it is quite possible for him to repeat it, and yet he refrains from doing so because he has repented—for example, a man cohabited unlawfully with a woman and after a time found himself alone with her again and he still loves her and is still as healthy as ever and it takes place in the same province in which he had previously sinned with her, and yet he refrains from repeating the transgression—he is a true penitent.

Of course, ideally we'd all be able to follow the advice of Warren Beatty, who asserted, "I am not going to make the same mistake once."[19] But of course, we do make mistakes. Or more accurately, in reality, none of us actually make the same mistake twice. The first time was a mistake. The second time was a choice.

Remember what Al Franken wrote: "Mistakes are a part of being human. Appreciate your mistakes for what they are: precious life lessons that can only be learned the hard way. Unless it's a fatal mistake, which, at least, others can learn from."[20]

TRUST

Trust nobody.

> —Tupac Shakur

A while back I received a catalog that featured a wristwatch lie detector. Listen to what it promised: "Negotiators can use this watch in order to determine when the other side is really making its last offer. Purchasing agents can use it to confirm that they are really getting the best price from their suppliers. Journalists can use it to evaluate the validity of the information they receive." And then the advertisement really gets attractive: "A wife can use it when her husband comes home late at night and says that he has been at a meeting … an employer can use it when he wants to find out if his salesman has been padding his expense account … if a salesman raves about the size of the discount he's offering you, just flash your watch at him and see what happens."

Should I buy a watch (just $79.95!) that can do all these things? I don't think so! This watch is a sign of the times, an example of the climate of suspicion in which we all live. Instead of loving each other, we are all involved in protecting ourselves from each other! We have gone from Johnny Carson's 1950s TV program *Who Do You Trust?* to the rap icon Tupac Shakur's "Trust nobody."

Those words of his you can find on the internet emblazoned on more than forty T-shirts, several iPhone cases, shower curtains, notebooks, and even masks. "Trust nobody" has become a battle cry for today.

The October 2020 issue of *The Atlantic* magazine featured an article by David Brooks entitled "America Is Having a Moral Convulsion."[21] His opening words are bleak: "Levels of trust in this country—in our institutions, in our politics, and in one another—are in a precipitous decline. And when social trust collapses, nations fail. Can we get it back before it's too late?" He makes his point with these statistics:

In 2012, 40 percent of Baby Boomers believed that most people can be trusted, as did 31 percent of members of Generation X. In contrast, only 19 percent of Millennials said most people can be trusted. Seventy-three percent of adults under 30 believe that "most of the time, people just look out for themselves," according to a Pew survey from 2018. Seventy-one percent of those young adults say that most people "would try to take advantage of you if they got a chance."

Many young people look out at a world they believe is screwed up and untrustworthy in fundamental ways. A mere 10 percent of Gen Zers trust politicians to do the right thing. Millennials are twice as likely as their grandparents to say that families should be able to opt out of vaccines. Only 35 percent of young people, versus 67 percent of old people, believe that Americans respect the rights of people who are not like them. Fewer than a third of Millennials say America is the greatest country in the world, compared to 64 percent of members of the Silent Generation.

In Brooks's words, "Americans today experience more instability than at any period in recent memory—fewer children growing up in married two-parent households, more single-parent households, more depression, and higher suicide rates."

There is much that has changed in America from the baby boomers to Generation X to millennials. Much has changed for the better. But not everything! America used to believe in community, in a shared destiny. If you needed help, you could knock on the door of the family next door. If you had to go on an errand, you could leave your child with a neighbor. Not anymore! Now there seems to be a continuous stream of stories about children being kidnapped or murdered. And in some cases, the crime was committed by the man next door. And so now nobody can trust their neighbor. Many of us have never even spoken to our next-door neighbors. We end up talking more to strangers on the internet than we do to real human beings. From "Love thy neighbor as thyself," we've gone to "Suspect thy neighbor."

And this is true not only in regard to your next-door neighbor but also even closer to home. A survey showed that 61 percent of Americans find it difficult to find someone to love. Remember when there was that computer virus called the Love Bug, or ILOVEYOU? We were told not to send a message to anybody with "I love you" as the subject line. And we were warned not to open any attachments titled "Love letter for you" or similar. Well, that's the way many people are living their lives these days. No attachments! No one to say "I love you" to!

During the last decade, fewer people have chosen to get married, maybe because they see too great a risk of heartbreak and divorce. Those who do marry might wonder if they should negotiate a prenuptial agreement, whether they should avoid being too trusting, whether they should hold off on having children because they might not be able to afford them.

The fact of the matter is if you are afraid to risk your heart and make a commitment, you will always find reasons to be afraid and reasons not to make a commitment.

Leo Buscaglia was right on target when he wrote this poem:
But risks must be taken because
the greatest hazard in life is to risk nothing.
The person who risks nothing,
does nothing, has nothing, is nothing.
He may avoid suffering and sorrow,
But he cannot learn, feel, change, grow or live.
Chained by his servitude he is a slave
who has forfeited all freedom.
Only a person who risks is free.

So the question is this: How can we restore our trust in one another? Simple. By learning from the porcupines!

The psychiatrist Bruno Bettelheim, commenting on a famous metaphor explained by philosopher Arthur Schopenhauer, wrote something that has always fascinated me. He noted that scientists often try to understand human nature by studying guinea pigs or rats or mice. Bettelheim believed that was a big mistake. If you really want to understand human nature, he said, you should study porcupines. Why? Because porcupines live out in the forest, and it is cold there in the wintertime, and so they huddle together to get warm. But what happens when they huddle together? They hurt each other with their quills. So they recoil. What happens when they recoil? They get cold from the weather. And so they alternate back and forth between being too far apart and the pain that brings and being too close and the pain that brings! And that is the way human beings are too.[22]

How does a porcupine make love? This sounds like a silly question, but it's not. How does a porcupine make love? *Very* carefully! Especially if they were hurt the first time.

And so it is with us. At times, friends can break our hearts, and it is hard to love and trust and reach out again after we have been hurt. Members of our families to whom we have given our hearts can disappoint us, change on us, divorce us, die on us. And whenever that happens, we will be tempted to recoil and withdraw. But if we do that for too long, we freeze.

We all make decisions in life that we regret. Unable to turn back the clock, we lose confidence in ourselves and turn inward and sullen. But if you do that too long, you will be frozen stiff. The reality is we're not safe even if we withdraw from everyone else because we are perfectly capable of breaking our own hearts. Of hurting ourselves. And when that happens and the cold sweeps down on us, it will be our connections with other people that sustain us. And so if we recognize how important it is to have family and friends to help and bolster us—if we have enough confidence in ourselves and recognize that no one is perfect, that no one gets it right all the time—perhaps we will accept the fact that it is worth the risk of reaching out to new opportunities, worth taking the chance to trust others and ourselves. After all, if the porcupines can do it, then so can we! The alternative, which is no alternative at all, is to live in a cold, cruel, and lonely world.

Joseph Stalin once said, "I trust no one, not even myself."

Similarly, Benito Mussolini has been quoted as saying, "It's good to trust others, but not to do so is better." We know where such mindsets led them and their people.

Contrast that to the words of Nelson Mandela in a press conference with then-president Bill Clinton: "I am not going to betray the trust of those who helped us."[23] This attitude of trust led to reconciliation for the South African people.

Remember the words of Billy Joel:
It's hard when you are always afraid.
You just recover when another belief is betrayed.
So break my heart if you must.
It's a matter of trust.

RIGHT AND WRONG

When I am right, I get angry. Churchill gets angry when
he is wrong. We are angry at each other much of the time.
—French President Charles de Gaulle

According to a 2020 Pew Research Center poll, 71 percent of
Democrats do not want to date a Republican, and 50 percent of Republicans don't want their child to marry a Democrat.
Nearly half of Democrats feel the same about Republicans.[24] In
a 2017 opinion piece for *Harper's Bazaar*, author Jennifer Wright
discussed the ways in which married couples with opposing political viewpoints (specifically couples where one partner supported
Donald Trump) were trying to work things out.[25] Wright's own
solution, however, was rather stark: "If you saddle yourself with
someone who fundamentally does not share your values ... just
skip it! Get a divorce."

That's it! Get a divorce! That's just what our country is doing!
We're divorcing each other because of "irreconcilable differences."
And our differences seem to be all-encompassing:

globalism vs. nationalism
border walls or open borders

rights vs. responsibilities
religious principles or secular values
right-to-life or "own your body"
health needs vs. economic needs
social media or personal privacy
I vs. we

There have always been differences in the political arena. Democrat and Republican legislators used to fight in the US Capitol before going out and having drinks together! No more! About this age of "irreconcilable differences," political columnist Jonah Goldberg wrote, "You must think the other side hates you and you must hate them for it."[26]

Charles Krauthammer was acknowledged as one of the brightest minds of our time. When he passed away, one of the nicest tributes I read of him was from Andrew Sullivan, then writing for *New York* magazine:

I knew Charles Krauthammer for a long time, through the Reagan years all the way through Obama and Trump. Perhaps the most remarkable thing is that we remained friends, albeit distant from time to time, throughout. Being a dissident on the right, as I became—particularly in the new century—was to invite ostracism and obloquy from the mainstream conservative media. But not from Charles. It wasn't because we didn't have disagreements. We argued strenuously from the get-go. In the 1980s, I was against the Contras; he was for. I then found the Iran-Contra affair appalling; he found it defensible. I became a sharp critic of Israel, as it continued and intensified the settlements; Charles could not offer a single stray thought critical of the Jewish state. He opposed marriage equality at first—on the slippery-slope polygamy grounds; I rebutted him. Then, perhaps most profoundly, he argued for a special team of US forces to torture prisoners, and I pulled out all the stops to oppose him. We agreed on Trump (he regarded his Russian ties as sinister), but even then, I found Charles's inability to disown the GOP baffling. I don't regret any of those positions now, and I doubt Charles ever did either. But he seemed incapable of personal abuse, animosity, or rhetorical demonization.[27] Let me repeat that last sentence. "He seemed incapable of personal abuse, animosity, or rhetorical demonization." That is too rarely the way it is in today's America! I grew up in an America where Republicans and Democrats worked with each other and, most importantly, compromised with each other for the good of the country. I grew up in a United States that had Rockefeller Republicans and Jackson Democrats, a country where there was no rigidity or rejection of every opinion but your own. Now that's gone. Now too many people seem unable to even recognize where the other side is coming from.

And this rigidity is not just when it comes to politics. It's developed in most every arena where we disagree with each other. As Senator Daniel Moynihan purportedly said, "You are entitled to your opinion, but you are not entitled to your own facts."[28] That is not true anymore! Now, because we are so sure of ourselves, we even differ on what, in fact, are the facts! Whereas in days gone by, we would argue about who should have been elected president, now we disagree on who was elected president! Sergeant Joe Friday (from television and radio's popular *Dragnet* series of the fifties and sixties) will long be remembered for his trademark comment: "Just the facts, ma'am."

Professor Daniel Kahneman, an Israeli and a Nobel Prize winner in economics, coined the phrase *illusion of validity*.[29] We are often so sure of ourselves and have such faith in our "facts" and opinions that we overlook hard data that contradict what we believe to be true and reject arguments that don't agree with our preconceptions. We operate under an illusion that we are right and opposing views (and even opposing facts) are definitely wrong.

How did we get to this point? Perhaps it was because we didn't listen to the words of King Solomon, who tells us in the book of Ecclesiastes, "Do not be overly righteous or excessively wise … Be not overly wicked nor a fool" (7:16). There's an obvious question here. One can understand King Solomon's admonition that one not be "overly wicked" or "a fool." It's bad enough to be wicked; one certainly shouldn't be overly wicked and act like a fool. But what about the first verse, the one that tells us not to be "overly righteous or excessively wise"? Sure, too much of anything is no good. But when it comes to piety, more would certainly seem better than less. And excessively wise—is that really possible? Is that such a terrible thing?

The answer might be that if a person is overly wicked, at least there's the possibility that one day they will realize that and they will repent and change. But if a person is overly righteous or excessively smart, they will think they're always right. There is no chance of them ever seeing when they're wrong or when they're overdoing it. There's no chance of them ever seeing anyone being right except for themselves.

There is an old Jewish joke that everybody knows; we've all heard it, and we have told it many times. I need only start it, and every one of you can supply the punch line. It is the story about two people who come to their rabbi with a dispute. The first one tells his side, and he argues so persuasively that the rabbi says to him, "You're right." Then the other person tells his side, and he, too, argues so persuasively that the rabbi says to him, "You're right."

The rabbi's wife is listening, and at this point she loses her patience, and she says to her husband, "Idiot! They are saying opposite things! They can't *both* be right!"

The rabbi thinks about what she is saying, and then he says to her, "You're right."

How come we know this story? How come we have all heard it and told it so often? Because it contains an important truth, which is this: the truth is often triple-sided. What that joke says in a way is that most of the disputes we have been engaged in are disputes between people who are partly right and people who are partly wrong. The percentages may vary from case to case, but this principle is still true. And therefore, what we ought to do is lower the decibels of our yelling at each other and listen to each other instead. For if we do, we just might learn from each other as well as teach each other. There really are two (or more) sides to every story.

It would be well to take to heart the words of a great sixteenth-century rabbinic scholar known as the Maharal of Prague, who once wrote, "If the thing is impure, it is impossible that it will not have some purity within it. Likewise, if the thing is pure, it is impossible that it will not have within it some impurity." Yes, there's some purity and impurity in each and every one of us. None of us are always wrong! And none of us are always right!

Remember what film producer Samuel Goldwyn said: "I'm willing to admit that I may not always be right, but I am never wrong."[30]

Smile! You're on Candid Camera!

Every breath you take
Every move you make
Every bond you break
Every step you take
I'll be watching you

—The Police

Seventeen-year-old Darnella Frazier made history when she stood for ten minutes filming as Derek Chauvin had his knee on the neck of George Floyd, who was lying on the pavement. This recording led to Chauvin's conviction and caused our country to confront issues that we can no longer turn our heads from. We saw it right before our eyes, and it could no longer be denied. You have to wonder if Derek Chauvin would have acted differently if he had known that his actions would go public. Jewish tradition seems to think so!

In the biblical book of Ruth we read how one day, searching for food in a time of famine, Ruth meets a true gentleman named Boaz who generously "gave her parched corn, and she ate and she was satisfied and had some left over" (2:14). And on these words our tradition, while recognizing the generosity of Boaz, still goes on to say, "Had Boaz known that the Bible would eternally record that he gave Ruth some parched grain to eat, he would have given her a royal banquet." Yes, Boaz, you didn't realize it, but your actions were being recorded. Sure it was nice that you gave Ruth something to eat … but you probably would have given a lot more than "parched corn" if you knew people would be reading about it until the end of time. If only you had realized it, you would have acted differently. It's not just Derek Chauvin … it's all of us in our day-to-day existence whose words and actions are being recorded.

This thought is poignantly made clear in a completely different context in a poem by Mary Rita Schilke Korzan called "When You Thought I Wasn't Looking":

When you thought I wasn't looking
You hung my first painting on the refrigerator
And I wanted to paint another.

When you thought I wasn't looking
You fed a stray cat
And I thought it was good to be kind to animals.

When you thought I wasn't looking
You baked a birthday cake just for me
And I knew that little things were special things.

When you thought I wasn't looking
You said a prayer
And I believed there was a God that I could always talk to.

When you thought I wasn't looking
You kissed me goodnight
And I felt loved.

When you thought I wasn't looking
I saw tears come from your eyes
And I learned that sometimes things hurt
But that it's all right to cry.

When you thought I wasn't looking
You smiled
And it made me want to look that pretty too.

When you thought I wasn't looking
You cared
And I wanted to be everything I could be.

When you thought I wasn't looking
I looked
And I wanted to say thanks
For all the things you did
When you thought I wasn't looking.[31]

The poem makes a very important point. Whether we know it or not, we're no different from Derek Chauvin. Everything we say and do is being recorded by our friends, our students, our neighbors, our rabbis and teachers—everyone. All of this and so much more is being "recorded" in the hearts and minds of everyone we interact with. We don't need a Darnella Frazier filming us to make our deeds known—they are known by the people all around us. And we don't even realize it!

And I'm not just talking about the "big" things. My mother died fifteen years ago, and yet, to this day, my brothers and I still reminisce about something my mother did that came so naturally to her that I don't even know if she was aware she was doing it! I don't even know if she realized that we—her children—saw what she was doing and what an impact it was making upon us. It was something she did when she thought we weren't looking. Every morning she would wake up early and put our underwear on the radiator so it would be warm when we got dressed! No big deal? God Almighty, what a big deal it was! What it said to us, how it made us feel, what it meant to us … can never—and will never—be forgotten.

What image of ourselves are we creating in people's minds when we think they aren't looking?

Remember these words from the *Ethics of the Fathers*: "All of your deeds are being recorded in a book."

THINGS

I don't cry for things that won't cry for me.

—Elizabeth Taylor

There is yin and yang, Republicans and Democrats, and a lot of other "opposites," some of which attract, while others fight like cats and dogs. Our society seems torn between "accumulate" and "declutter."

On the one hand, we are obsessed with possessions and with material things. Just ask Kanye West. Upon his divorce from Kim Kardashian, he had to pack up and move his five hundred pairs of sneakers from their house.

Many of us raise our kids to think this way, to think that "things" are very important. If not to them, then certainly to us.

There was a *Wall Street Journal* headline that really struck me: "Italian Firm Fashions a Look Tailor-Made for Indulgent Parents."[32] The article reported on a company named Pinco that had designed a line of children's clothes that was catching on like wildfire in America. Dresses for six-year-olds cost over $600, with $200 hand-bags to match. The target audience? Listen! "Mothers, who in the words of the buyers thronging the Pinco booth, regard their children as fashion accessories." That's what we've turned our kids into!

31

Fashion accessories!

Our attachment to things has led us to create a world so unlike the world of King David that (as one anonymous online wit asserted) he'd probably have written a very different version of the twenty-third psalm if he were writing today.

> The Lord is my shepherd, I shall not want.
> He leadeth me to Neiman Marcus.
> He giveth me energy for shopping.
> He restoreth my checkbook.
> He teacheth me to make restaurant reservations.
> He leadeth me past Kmart for mine own sake.
> Yea, though I walk by Target,
> I shall not go in, for Thou art with me.
> Thy fashionable clothes, they comfort me.
> Thou preparest diamond jewelry for me in the presence of mine enemies.
> Thou anointest my face with Chanel cosmetics.
> My cup overflows.
> Surely designer clothes shall follow me to the end of my days,
> And I will walk on Rodeo Drive forever. Amen.[33]

But perhaps a new generation has arrived, one with a very different focus. This new focus was reflected in a *Washington Post* article headlined "Who Dies with the Most Toys Now Loses."[34] We now live in an age of decluttering, brought to us all the way from Japan via Marie Kondo's bestselling book *The Life-Changing Magic of Tidying Up: The Japanese Art of Decluttering and Organizing.* There is even a book titled *Decluttering for Dummies*! Still, you don't have to be a dummy to realize that almost everything we have in our closets, cabinets, and basements, we really don't need—and never needed! The items of clothing we never wear, the trinkets we have in boxes large and small, the things we could not pass up because they were on sale ... all these and much more have got to go. That's the wisdom of our day. It certainly beats having to pack up five hundred pairs of sneakers!

Writing on the website CalmMoment.com, Ruby Deevoy explained that accumulating stuff is a very human habit, albeit an outdated one. "Over the years, many scientists have theorized that the pull to buy and store things we don't need, or even really want, stems from a natural and adaptive instinct run amok: to hoard food, furs, and all of those essential-for-survival things that are simply not essential anymore. As a result, we are still compelled to gather but rather than fulfilling a need, we are now left feeling stressed, unable to focus, and unsatisfied."[35]

Remember what David Rockefeller wrote? "I am convinced that material things can contribute a lot to making one's life pleasant, but, basically, if you do not have very good friends and relatives who matter to you, life will be really empty and sad and material things cease to be important."

I don't know if I agree. Some "things" are very meaningful and important. Everyone has some souvenirs, mementoes, trinkets that are precious. It can even be something as seemingly worthless as a Maxwell House Haggadah. Let me tell you a story I once came across in a magazine about a woman named Phyllis Horowitz.

When Phyllis Horowitz got divorced, her in-laws didn't ask her to give back the Rosenthal china or sterling silver flatware they had given to her when she had married their son. But they did insist that she return the wine-stained Maxwell House Haggadahs that had been in the Horowitz family for forty years. Phyllis returned the Haggadahs because she understood the sentimental value they had for the Horowitz family. As she put it, "They were used at family Seders on the Lower East Side and later when the family lived in Brooklyn. When we bought our home on Long Island, my in-laws stopped making Seders, and I was given the Haggadahs. Now that I'm divorced and my in-laws are retiring to Florida, the Haggadahs will be heading south."

If you think about it, every family has a treasure like the Horowitz family's Maxwell House Haggadahs. But not everything is to be valued and cherished. Malcolm Forbes said, "He who dies with the most toys wins." Well, Forbes happened to have quite a substantial toy collection, and when he died, his children sold the collection! Was that winning?

Elizabeth Taylor wrote a book entitled *My Love Affair with Jewelry.* She was robbed. Thieves broke into her safe-deposit box and stole her jewelry (which I imagine was quite a lot—she had six engagement rings!). At the time of the robbery, reporters asked her, "Did you cry?"

Remember what she answered: "I don't cry for things that won't cry for me."

GOD

God don't make no mistakes. That's how He got to be God.

—Archie Bunker, *All in the Family*

Since COVID-19 enveloped the world, people have studied, analyzed, and debated what caused it. But a common theme for many—particularly religious people—is that God brought this plague upon us because of our sins. And what were those sins? That depends on what you believe.

Rick Wiles, an evangelical minister, warned his congregation, "Stay out of those synagogues … there's a plague in them. God is dealing with false religions. God is dealing with people who oppose his son, Jesus Christ." God is punishing the world for the sins of the Jews? Couldn't Reverend Wiles have come up with something a little more original? That one is so old!

A Muslim imam at least was more inclusive. He blamed it on both the Jews and the Christians, whose rejection of Muhammed as the Prophet of God has raised God's anger and requires retribution.

Then there are homosexuals. For some religious leaders, it's always their fault! Rabbi Meir Mazuz claimed that the LGBTQ community and gay-pride marches went against nature and had caused the coronavirus pandemic.

So God did it! He caused more than two million people across the globe to die because of the sins of the Jews, the Christians, the homosexuals … or whomever else you don't like!

The problem with this is that a truly religious person would know that's not how God sees Himself. It's right there in Exodus 34:6–7.

> God, God is gracious and compassionate,
> Patient and abounding in kindness and faithfulness,
> Assuring love for a thousand generations,
> Forgiving iniquity, transgression and sin,
> And granting pardon.

So what's the word on God? Good God or bad God? Compassionate or avenging? The question is not new! The Enlightenment, a time of great philosophical questioning in the eighteenth and nineteenth centuries, was in a sense spurred on by this question. In 1755, an earthquake hit Lisbon, Portugal, destroying many of the churches while Lisbon's priests attempted to salvage the crucifixes and religious icons that had been intended to ward off the catastrophe. But it didn't help. Nearly a hundred thousand people were killed, many while praying in or fleeing from churches. To top it all off, the earthquake occurred on All Saints' Day. And to add insult to injury, while most every major church was destroyed, at the brothels in Lisbon's red-light district, it was business as usual! How could God allow that to happen? Great minds like Voltaire and Kant couldn't comprehend it!

But the Talmud does! The sages in the Talmud taught us, "Nature follows its own course." The brothels survived and the churches were destroyed not because of God but because the brothels were built on higher, more stable ground!

The great prophet Isaiah spoke for all of us when he wrote, "'For my thoughts are not your thoughts, neither are your ways my ways,' sayeth the Lord. 'As the heavens are higher than the earth, so are my ways higher'" (Isaiah 55:8–9).

In the powerful Broadway show *Agnes of God*, a court-appointed psychiatrist reveals to the Mother Superior why she abandoned her faith. As a young girl, her best friend had died in a horrible car accident. A nun at her Catholic school had explained why it had happened: "She didn't say her morning prayers that day, so God punished her." Instead of inculcating the desired fear that would produce a lifelong devotee of prayer, the "explanation" had created revulsion as well as abhorrence for a God who could be so cruel in response to a little child's forgetfulness. The playwright had the good sense to make the Mother Superior respond, "What a stupid woman!"[36]

We don't understand God's ways. We understand only our ways. And what are our ways? Maimonides, the great twelfth-century Jewish thinker, said that when evil befalls mankind, it's for one of three reasons: One, because of circumstances our body is subjected to, by which he meant genes and DNA and tumors. Two, because of things we do to others, such as wars. Or three, by the harm we do to ourselves by our own actions. Maimonides said that this third reason is the most common. Yes, it's not what God does to us; it's what we do to ourselves! That is the way God made this world work. What role does God play? Next time you talk to him, ask him. God is there to comfort, support, sustain, and uplift you. At the same time, "God helps those who help themselves."

Remember what Bob Hope said: "If I'm on the course and lightning starts, I get inside fast. If God wants to play through, let him."

BUILDING IDENTITY

BEAUTY

Beauty? Let me tell you something: being thought of as a beautiful woman has spared me nothing in life. No heartache, no trouble. Love has been difficult.

—Halle Berry

I t's referred to as the *Zoom boom*—during the pandemic, plastic surgeons around the world were reporting a major increase in requests for procedures.

Jon Mendelsohn, medical director of Advanced Cosmetic Surgery & Laser Center in Cincinnati, said injectable procedures such as Botox and fillers were up 90 percent compared with the same period the previous year. The *Washington Post* quoted Jason Champagne, a plastic surgeon in Beverly Hills, California, who said many people focus on their chin, jawline, and neck on Zoom because the camera angles tend to accentuate those features. "We are not accustomed to seeing ourselves while in conversation with others, so people are paying attention to their facial movements and features while speaking," Champagne said.[37]

How pervasive is this? Well, a Miami plastic surgeon has written a children's book explaining why Mommy is getting a nose job or breast implants. *My Beautiful Mommy*, written by Dr. Michael

Salzhauer, depicts a mom telling her daughter that she will look different after she comes home from her surgery.

"Why are you going to look different?" the daughter asks.

Mom responds, "Not just different, my dear—prettier." Dr. Salzhauer said he targeted the book to children ages four to seven.[38]

Now, the words *nip* and *tuck* are nothing new. They even served as the title for a popular TV drama, *Nip/Tuck*, which ran for seven seasons. But did you know the show's theme song was entitled "A Perfect Lie"?

One can understand the desire to look good. One can understand the desire not to look "too old." But how far must we go? And how young must we start? We live in an era where the *New York Times* headlined an article "How Young Is Too Young to Have a Nose Job and Breast Implants?"[39]

Another manifestation of this quest for beauty is found in the endless diet programs and products. Statistics show that one-third of twelve- and thirteen-year-olds are actively trying to lose weight by dieting, vomiting, using laxatives, or taking diet pills. Those are twelve-year-olds. And adults are no better! The desire to be thin is so powerful that people would die for it! I read an article about a survey in which 15 percent of women and 11 percent of men said that they would give up more than five years of their lives to be their desired weight.[40]

How sad it is to be so beauty conscious. Halle Berry, arguably one of the most beautiful people in the world, said, "Beauty is essentially meaningless and is always transitory."[41]

Perhaps even more telling are the words of Israel's immortal leader Golda Meir, who once said, "Not being beautiful was the true blessing. Not being beautiful forced me to develop my inner resources. The pretty girl has a handicap to overcome."[42] Perhaps that's why the description of the ideal beautiful woman in the Song of Songs is one whose "neck is like the Tower of David" (Song of Sg. 4:4) while the ideal man is one whose "legs are pillars of marble" (Song of Sg. 5:15). The writer obviously didn't have Twiggy in mind!

The modern obsession with thinness would seem strange to many previous generations. A Talmudic reference to two great sages, Yishmael ben Yossi and Elazer ben Shimon, mentions that they had such enormously protruding stomachs that as they stood facing each other with their stomachs touching, a pair of oxen could pass between them. And then the Talmud adds that their wives were even heavier! In *Fiddler on the Roof,* Tevye's "If I Were a Rich Man" fantasy of Golde is that she would look "like a rich man's wife, with a proper double chin." Indeed, King Solomon's chapter in the book of Proverbs describing the "woman of valor" has a lesson for all of us (especially when we consider that such a woman might be ridiculed in our day and age). The woman of valor is praised for her intelligence, her managerial skills, her lack of vanity, and her devotion. She is called "more precious than rubies," and there's not a word about how she looks.

We would all do well to keep in mind the words of Coco Chanel, a woman who knew quite a bit about appearance: "You can be beautiful at thirty, charming at forty, and irresistible for the rest of your life."[43] She knew that a person need not be beautiful to be compelling, charming, and fascinating. If only more of us would embrace that truth!

Remember what Redd Foxx said: "Beauty is only skin deep, but ugly goes all the way to the bone!"[44]

PLAY BY THE RULES

Only the little people pay taxes.

—Leona Helmsley

L eona Helmsley, daughter of immigrants, rose to fame and fortune as a businesswoman and hotelier. When she died on August 20, 2007, she left behind an estate estimated to be worth more than $4 billion, including a $12 million trust fund for her dog named Trouble. Yet despite her enormous wealth, Leona Helmsley, nicknamed the Queen of Mean, served a term in prison for three counts of tax evasion, three counts of filing false personal tax returns, sixteen counts of assisting in the filing of false corporate and partnership tax returns, and ten counts of mail fraud.

When you think about it, what she did makes no sense. I mean, I can understand someone who is very poor and needs to feed his family feeling the urge to cheat the government for money. I can understand it although certainly not condone it. I can understand someone getting involved in a business deal with the best of intentions and then, as it progresses, finding that there's something shady about it but fearing that if they pull out now, their life savings may go down the tube. I can understand but not condone. But with Leona Helmsley, I don't understand it! It was so unnecessary … so ridiculous. Why did she do it?

45

I think, without even knowing it, she herself provided the most honest answer. During the trial, her housekeeper quoted her as saying, "Only the little people pay taxes."[45] Those words are more than a statement; they are a mindset. What was Leona Helmsley really saying? She was saying that some of us reach a point where we are so wealthy, so powerful, that we don't have to play by the rules. The rules don't apply to me! I can make my own rules! Aristotle Onassis said it all: "The only rule is that there are no rules!"[46]

I think this explains the behavior of many people.

It explains the behavior of Hedy Lamarr, who probably had more than enough money on which to live and yet who got caught shoplifting over and over again. I guess she figured that if she was rich and famous, then the rules didn't apply to her.

It explains the behavior of Columba Bush. Her husband, Jeb Bush, makes a fairly good living, and yet she lied on the customs form when her plane landed in Miami. She tried to get away with bringing some jewelry into this country without declaring it at customs. Did she really need to do that? Did she really need to save the few dollars she would have paid in taxes? Instead, she ended up on the front page of every newspaper in the country, to the embarrassment of her husband and her brother-in-law, who was then president of the United States. The only explanation that I can think of for what she did is that she must have thought the rules didn't apply to her.

It explains the behavior of Ivan Boesky, the stock speculator who pleaded guilty to insider trading. I suppose he thought the rules didn't apply to him.

It explains the behavior of Michael Milkin, the junk-bond king, who served twenty-two months in prison and paid a $200 million fine for violating U.S. securities laws. He could afford to pay a fine of $200 million … so why didn't he play by the rules? Obviously, because he felt the rules did not apply to him.

And you know what? All this explains, to some degree, the behavior of a man who cheats on his wife or who spends a fortune on his drug habit, just for the sake of doing something that he knows is forbidden. For such men, it may not be the money, and it may not be the sex. It may just be the exhilarating feeling of being able to say, "The rules that apply to everyone else don't apply to me."

If only King David had understood this. King David, who had six wives and who knows how many concubines, nevertheless reached out and took the wife of one of his soldiers. I guess he thought that the rules did not apply to him. As a result of that mistake, the whole life of King David took a terrible turn. Until then, God loved David, the people loved David, everyone loved David. But from that day on, the life of David went straight downhill. And he learned, the hard way, that the rules that apply to everyone else applied to him too.

How much happier we all would be if we always lived by the rules. I remember once hearing that the Internal Revenue Service received an envelope with a thousand dollars in cash, together with an anonymous note that read, "I am sending you this money because I have not been able to sleep. If I still can't sleep after this, I'll send you the rest that I owe you." Ask yourself this: Wouldn't it be nice to go to sleep at night with no fear of getting caught hanging over you? What a blessing to be like Henry Wadsworth Longfellow's village blacksmith, who "looks the whole world in the face, / For he owes not any man."[47]

Remember what Tiger Woods said: "I knew my actions were wrong. But I convinced myself that normal rules didn't apply ... I thought I could get away with whatever I wanted to. I felt that I had worked hard my entire life and deserved to enjoy all the temptations around me. I felt I was entitled ... I was wrong, I was foolish. I don't get to play by different rules. The same boundaries that apply to everyone apply to me."[48]

CAREERS

I blew it!

—Sam Walton

Those were the last words Sam Walton—founder of Walmart—uttered before passing. "I blew it!" This, despite the fact that at the time of his death, he was worth $65 billion.

About Sam Walton's final words, business journalist Mike Michalowicz wrote, "Sam Walton blew it? How could that be? He was a full-time, always-there businessman! He would do anything to grow his business, and it gave him immense fame and fortune! But that's where the problem lies because when it came to the rest of his life, Sam wasn't nearly as dedicated. He was never really 'there' as a father, husband and friend. He had the wealthiest pockets, but the poorest soul. And in those last minutes of his life, he realized where he had failed."[49]

Think about it. Ask someone what they do, and see if they begin by telling you that they've been married for twenty-three years, or see if they tell you that they have two boys and a girl, or see if they tell you that they volunteer for Big Brothers Big Sisters of America or are very charitable. Instead, what do you guess they are most likely to say? Most probably they'll define themselves by their job or by profession. They will say "I'm a stockbroker" or "I'm a lawyer" or "I'm a doctor" or "I work for IBM." Work is their identity. When you ask someone who they are, they tell you what they do for a living, as if that's all that defines a person, as if that's all that makes you who you are.

And what if you are retired? What do you say? Is the only way you can identify yourself by saying, "I used to be a … "?

As Peggy Lee asked, "Is that all there is?" I guess not, if you asked Sam Walton. And it's not just him! More than one prominent, successful entrepreneur or public figure has asserted the importance of family over work. For example, former United Nations ambassador John Danforth surprised everyone when he took early retirement. His spokesman, Richard Grenell, explained, "In November he said to me that there are many people who can be United States ambassador to the UN, but there is only one person who can be Sally Danforth's husband."[50]

Think of the painful words of former US surgeon general Dr. oycelyn Elders. She was supposed to help Americans learn how to live healthy lives. And then her twenty-eight-year-old son, Kevin, was sentenced to ten years in prison for selling cocaine. In a letter to the sentencing judge, Dr. Elders wrote that when her son needed her most, she was too busy with politics. "As I sat there watching my son, I thought of how much and how long he had suffered because at the time of his greatest need, we had not been able to communicate as a family. I was too busy with my confirmation hearings."[51] Hillary Clinton, who spent a good many years of her life in public life, was smart enough to say, "Don't confuse having a career with having a life."

That on some level we all know what really matters is obvious when you go to a cemetery and look at the headstones. You will see carved into the stone the deceased's name and date of death and sometimes their date of birth as well. And then often there are a few other words about who that person was. But I have never seen the person's profession written there. Listed instead are words describing the deceased as being a "devoted spouse" or "loving parent" or "beloved child." If that's the way we are to be remembered, why not spend more time embracing those parts of our identity while we are alive?

We should not wait until death claims us before we own what really counts in our lives—that our connections with others are what tell us who we are. Smart (and lucky ... or both) are those who understand that early enough to live into that truth.

David Williams played tackle for the Houston Oilers football team. In 1993, he did something that was on page one of all the newspapers for a day or two, and then it was forgotten. But it shouldn't have been. His wife gave birth to their first child on a Sunday morning, the day his team was scheduled to play the New England Patriots in Massachusetts. Dave was present all during the delivery and went through the whole experience with his wife, and then the baby was born, and he had a choice. He could have arranged to get on a plane and arrived at the game in time to play, or he could have stayed with his wife. He chose to skip the game. So when his wife woke up, he was there. When his baby looked up for the first time, he was there. The Houston Oilers fined him $110,000 for missing the game. And that aroused a howl of protest.

The reporters asked Williams, "If you had known that you were going to be fined $110,000, would you still have done it?"

His answer was "Of course. Isn't family what the money's for?"[52] It wasn't enough for him to be there just for the delivery. He wanted those first moments of deepest joy, of intimate sharing, of bonding with his child. "Isn't family what the money's for?"

Warren Buffett, the Oracle of Omaha, knows a thing or two about money and success, so it wouldn't be surprising if he waxed lyrical about careers or income. And yet, in *The Snowball: Warren Buffett and the Business of Life,* author Alice Schroeder described a moment when he told a group of business school students, "Basically, when you get to my age, you'll really measure your success in life by how many of the people you want to have love you actually do love you. I know people who have a lot of money, and they get testimonial dinners, and they get hospital wings named after them ... but the truth is that nobody in the world loves them."[53]

If you still don't get it, hear these words Barbara Bush told the graduates at the 1990 Wellesley College commencement ceremony: "As important as your obligations as a doctor, lawyer, or business leader may be ... your human connections with spouses, with children, with friends, are the most important investment you will ever make. At the end of your life, you will never regret not having passed one more test, not winning one more verdict, or not closing one more deal. You will regret time not spent with a husband, child, friend, or a parent."[54]

Jeanie Buss, who inherited ownership of the Los Angeles Lakers basketball team from her father, Jerry, said of him, "My dad had his children, but the Lakers was his baby."[55]

Is that the way you want to be remembered?

Remember what Marilyn Monroe said: "A career is wonderful, but you can't curl up with it on a cold night."[56]

APPRECIATION

Even now, after all these years, maybe I need a boxing cornerman to give me a constant "We're doing okay, kid."

—Tony Curtis

In one episode of *The Apprentice*, Donald Trump is in his helicopter leaving a charity basketball game at Riverbank State Park when he laments, "No one came over to say goodbye to me." That was an early indication of what Trump would be like as president. His need for attention and affirmation meant starring in his own television show was not enough—nor was being president. Of course, he's not alone in his desire to be appreciated.

The fact is no matter how well known people are, they still want to be noticed, still want to be complimented, still need to feel needed. In this, they're like all of us. We all long to be reassured that we matter to someone, that our efforts are seen and valued. This isn't vanity either. It's not weakness (except maybe when taken to a Trump-like extreme). It's natural.

A woman once came to my office carrying a book that bore this inscription: "To my wife for all that you mean to me, for all that you do for me ... with all my love." It was signed with her husband's name. The woman showed this to me and immediately started to cry. When I asked why the tears, she replied, "My husband didn't write it. I did. He never has a good word to say to me. I needed to hear these words." Of course she needed that. We all do!

When deprived of that kind of appreciation, particularly for a long time and particularly from someone important like a partner or parent, some people put up defensive walls, declaring that they don't need validation from anyone. That might be true, for a few people at least, but I'd argue that it's not the healthiest expression of the human need for connection. As for the woman who came to see me, I admire her vulnerability. Writing that inscription took courage and honesty. She could at least admit to herself (and me) that those twenty or so words were something she deserved to hear. How much more valuable would they have been coming from her husband, and how easy it would have been for him to offer them.

We often criticize our children or partner "for their own good." Maybe it is useful to hear what they're doing wrong, to benefit from our wisdom, but why stop there? Why don't we compliment them for their own good? They might benefit as much (or even more!) from our acknowledgement of their successes, good qualities, and special gifts.

It's like the husband who complains that whenever he argues with his wife, she gets historical.

His friend replies, "You must mean *hysterical*."

And the man says, "No, she gets historical ... she remembers and throws back in my face every disagreement and everything I've ever done wrong."

I'm sure you recognize the temptation, even if it's not one you indulge in, to let a heated argument devolve into a list of every mistake from the start of the relationship onward. It feels pretty terrible to be on the receiving end of that kind of historical tirade, but it's equally damaging to be the one holding on to that list of (real or imagined) wrongs. Imagine if instead of being historical about the bad, we were historical about the good. How amazing would that be? I can't prove it, but it seems to me that the least-observed holiday on the world calendar is World Compliment Day, every March 1. The founder of World Compliment Day explained why he started it: "Nothing stimulates more, gives more energy, makes people happier and, as far as business is concerned, increases productivity and commitment faster than sincere appreciation. So why not use it a little bit more?"[57]

What's stopping us from actively praising those we love for what they do or simply who they are? Maybe it makes us feel vulnerable to be the one offering that kind of support. We might have grown up mistakenly believing that silence is strength or that kindness and control are incompatible. Admitting just how much we admire a person or expressing our need for them might feel risky at first, but it's a risk worth taking, and the potential rewards for everyone involved far outweigh the possible downsides. As Will Rogers once said, "Go home and say something nice to your wife, even if it shocks her at first."

Apparently, many psychological problems result from feelings of worthlessness. If that's true, think how transformative it will be if, every now and then, you tell your kid you think he's pretty great or your husband how much you liked the meal he cooked last night. And don't stop there! If you're fortunate enough to still have your parents, tell them as well! Getting older doesn't reduce our need to feel loved and appreciated. It can even increase it.

While you're at it, don't stop with your immediate family. In all our lives, there has been someone who (possibly without even realizing it) helped make us who we are today. For example, Bob

Greene is a well-known political columnist and author. A few years ago, in an op-ed article in the *Wall Street Journal*, he described how he was looking through a book of photographs he had saved from his youth when came across a picture of his first-grade teacher, Patty Ruoff. He wondered if she was still alive and if he could find her. Turns out, she was still alive, and she had never left the community where she had once taught grade school. He called her, and in his words, "I tried to explain to her why I was calling. I said that if I've ever written a graceful sentence, if I've ever appreciated a turn of phrase in a good book, if I've ever found comfort in a beautifully told story, it all began with her. I told her that hundreds of other boys and girls who once passed through her classroom likely have reason to be just as grateful. And I told her I was sure that many other men and women, now grown, must have called to thank her over the years. There was a slight pause, and then she said: 'No one ever has.'"[58]

Think about it! There are lots of people for whom you could be the first to let them know just what a profound impact they've had on your life. It's not hard to imagine how great they'd feel to hear that you remember them and acknowledge what they did for you.

Let me take it a step further and tell you about Charles Plumb—pilot, prisoner of war (POW), and now inspirational speaker whose story is told online.

Charles Plumb is a US Naval Academy graduate who flew fighter jets in the Vietnam conflict. After seventy-five combat missions, his plane was destroyed by a surface-to-air missile. Plumb parachuted into enemy hands and spent six years as a POW. He survived that ordeal and came home a hero.

One day, years later, Plumb and his wife were sitting in a restaurant when a man came up and said, "You're Plumb! You flew jet fighters in Vietnam, and you were shot down!"

"How in the world did you know that?" asked Plumb.

"I packed your parachute," the man replied. "I guess it worked!"

Plumb described how he couldn't sleep that night but lay awake, thinking about that man. He wondered how many times he, a respected fighter pilot, might have passed that "lowly" sailor, how many times he never said, "Hello," "Good morning," or "How are you." It grated on his conscience. Plumb imagined the many lonely hours the sailor must have spent carefully weaving the fabric together, making sure the parachute was just right, and going to great lengths to make it as precise as possible, knowing that somebody's life depended on it. Plumb now goes around the world as a motivational speaker, asking people to recognize who's packing their own parachute.

Who packed your parachute in life? Who were the people who reached out to you? Who has been there for you at a single crucial moment or continuously over the years? I'm talking about the teacher, friend, family member, doctor or orthodontist, housekeeper, employer, or classmate who at some point made all the difference in your life, helping make you who and what you are.

Why not reach out to that person? They will definitely appreciate knowing that they are appreciated. Imagine how uplifted you would feel to learn that you had packed someone else's parachute, that you had transformed their life—and that they had taken time to thank you for it.

Remember what James Caan said: "Actors have bodyguards and entourages, not because anyone wants to hurt them—who would want to hurt an actor?—but because they want to get recognized. God forbid someone doesn't recognize them. They'd have a fucking heart attack."[59]

CROWD CONTROL

A live concert, to me, is exciting because of all the electricity that is generated in the crowd and on stage. It's my favorite part of the business, live concerts.

—Elvis Presley

Every entertainer thrives on a crowd. During the COVID-19 pandemic, all professional sports shown on TV had profound rates of attrition. The game just isn't the same without the fans! An article in the *New Yorker* pointed out, "It's easy to forget that, in the theatre, each ticket buyer plays a role. The quality of our attention—silent or ecstatic, galled or bored—is a kind of free-standing, always-improvising character, and makes each in-person performance unrepeatable."[60]

It is not just entertainers and athletes who feel this way. In the book of Proverbs, we are told, "In multitudes there is glorification of the King of the Universe" (Prov. 14:28).

Yes, it's not just Elvis "The King" but the King of Kings who loves a crowd!

But that doesn't tell the whole story. In 1972, a social psychologist, Irving Janis, coined the term *groupthink*, a word that describes "when a group makes faulty decisions because group pressure leads to the formation of 'mental deficiency, reality testing and moral judgment.'"[61] Yes, sometimes we get so caught up in the crowd that we allow others to think for us, even when that thinking goes against our own inner beliefs. Groupthink, quite simply, is what happens when people start making decisions not based on analytic thinking but on the basis of what most of the group is thinking!

Think back to the scenes of the huge crowds that greeted Hitler and the Nazis ... the wild enthusiasm of the people caught up in the excitement of the moment. Right from the very beginning, it was those crowds, so completely swept up in Hitler's oratory, that meant the Final Solution of the Jewish problem was about to take place. William Shirer, the author of the monumental *The Rise and Fall of the Third Reich*, described in his diaries the first time he, as a reporter stationed in Germany, heard Adolf Hitler address a crowd of brown-shirted Germans. He wrote, "There in the floodlit night, jammed together like sardines, in one massive formation, the little men of Germany, who have made Nazism possible, achieved the highest state of being the Germanic man knows: the shedding of their individual souls and minds—with the personal responsibilities and doubts and problems—until under the mystic lights and at the sound of the magic words of the Austrian they were merged completely in the German herd."[62]

Please don't misunderstand! I am comparing no one and nothing to Hitler and the Nazis. There was an article in the *Wall Street Journal* entitled "'It's Kind of Like an Addiction': On the Road With Trump's Rally Diehards."[63] The article talked about Donald Trump's most devoted fans, some of whom drove more than a thousand miles to attend his rallies. Some have been to more than ten of them! These words really captured my attention: "All of them describe in different ways a euphoric flow of emotions between themselves and the president, a sort of adrenaline-fueled, psychic cleansing that follows ninety minutes of chanting and cheering with fifteen thousand other like-minded Trump junkies."

Or as one of these junkies, April Owens, said, "Once you start going, it's kind of like an addiction, honestly."

Now these were well-meaning people. The *Wall Street Journal* described some of them in these words: "Several of those with jobs live paycheck to paycheck, but constantly offer strangers a cold beverage, sandwiches, or their last cigarette." These are people for whom, as the article expressed it, "the Trump era marks their political awakening." Donald Trump gave them a voice. And that's good. But often the voice that is raised by a crowd can turn ugly and harmful; it did on January 6, 2021, when a mob invaded the US Capitol.

Little wonder that as far back as the first great work of political philosophy, Plato's *Republic*, we find a discussion of the evils of mob rule. The noted theologian Søren Kierkegaard has a famous essay "The Crowd is Untruth."[64] That ain't necessarily so!

To my mind, closer to the truth are the words of Albert Einstein: "The one who follows the crowd usually gets no further than the crowd. The one who walks alone is likely to find himself in places no one else has ever taken."[65]

In his bestselling book *Influence: The Psychology of Persuasion*, psychologist Robert Cialdini wrote, "Whether the question is what to do with an empty popcorn box in a movie theater, how fast to drive on a certain stretch of highway, or how to eat the chicken at a dinner party, the actions of those around us will be important in defining the answer."[66] But is that healthy—physically, spiritually, emotionally?

Remember what Margaret Thatcher said: "Don't follow the crowd; let the crowd follow you."[67]

SELF-IMAGE

I don't like to analyze myself because I might not like what I see.

—Donald Trump

The famous Hasidic master Rabbi Menachem Mendel of Kotzk used to interpret the biblical commandment "Thou shall not steal" as meaning "Thou shall not steal from thyself." Or in other words, don't delude yourself! We often lie to ourselves about our children, who and what they really are. We often lie to ourselves about our relationships with others. Often we are engaged in disagreements with others, thinking the worst of them, being unable to see that frequently we are the ones who are at fault.

Remember the following story? A senior citizen was driving down the freeway when his cell phone rang. Upon answering, he heard his wife's voice urgently warning him, "Herman, I just heard on the news that there's a car going the wrong way on Interstate 280. Please be careful."

"It's not just one car," said Herman. "I see hundreds of them!"

We even lie to ourselves about ourselves! If you picture yourself a certain way in your mind, after a while, you can begin to believe it's a true picture. Carl Bernstein of Watergate fame wrote a book about Hillary Clinton entitled *A Woman in Charge*. In it he wrote, "When it comes to herself, she sees with something less than candor and lucidity. She sees—like so many others—what she wants to see."[68]

And most of us are no different! Let's try this exercise: Stop and think for a moment. I want you to think of the first three words that come to mind in describing yourself. What are the first three things that come to mind about how you think you look when you see yourself in the mirror ? What do you see? Who are you? Are you kind, bright, haughty, generous, selfish, pretty? Go ahead. Think about it.

Now, I want you to pause again and take this "selfie": What are the first three things that you think people think of when they see you? How do they see you? Are they the same three words you chose to describe how you see yourself?

How right Robert Burns was when he wrote the following:
O wad some Pow'r the giftie gie us
To see oursels as ithers see us![69]

That is, "Oh would some Power give us the gift / To see ourselves as others see us." These lovely words come from a poem with the unlikely title of *To a Louse*. It tells of how Burns saw this fancy woman dressed in an expensive bonnet, and he observed she didn't realize that there was a louse crawling in it. Here is someone walking around, thinking about how great she looks to all the world, but what the world sees when looking at her is a louse crawling around. His point was simple: Wouldn't it be great if we could see ourselves through the eyes of others because we often don't see ourselves for what we really are?

To quote another great English writer, "To thine own self be true." Or let's update Shakespeare's wisdom: "To thine own selfie be true!"

So let me ask husbands and wives something specific: The three words that first came to mind to describe how you see yourself ... do you think there is any chance your spouse uses the same three words to describe how they see you? That is not what I hear in my office, whether we're discussing preparations for their child's bar or bat mitzvah or talking about issues in the family. In most every instance, the differences between husband and wife are not simply that one thinks they are right and the other is wrong. It's more a matter of each one having no idea of how they are coming across. Maybe one is incapable of seeing that there might be another side to the issue—or even that they themselves just might be the problem! Or maybe one is coming across as a total know-it-all without even knowing it.

Yes, often we are not as innocent and pure as we make ourselves out to be. And yes, often we are not as bad and as persecuted as we think we are.

But knowing thyself, telling the truth to yourself about yourself, is the most important quality for change and growth.

Remember what John le Carré wrote: "People are very secretive—secret even from themselves."

To Have and to Hold

MARRIAGE

When you're in love, it's the most glorious two and a half days of your life.

—Richard Lewis

I know a rabbi who recently celebrated his fortieth wedding anniversary, and when a congregant asked him what the key was to the success of his marriage, he replied, "My wife and I agreed long ago that no matter how busy we were, no matter what our professional obligations, once a week—no matter what—we would go out to dinner. She went on Wednesdays, and I went on Mondays!"

Let's be honest. No matter how many years you've been married, whether one or sixty, how many of us can honestly say, "This person is exactly who I wanted … exactly who I thought I was getting"?

Not me! My wife and I grew up living two blocks away from each other. We hung out in the same social circles. We thought we really knew each other! And then we got married and discovered many, many things.

I like to drive fast, Sherry slow.

I like the television loud, Sherry low.

On the radio, she prefers NPR; I choose classic rock.

She likes the air-conditioning high; I like it low.

I like the heat high, she low!

One of us is a spender, the other a saver.

One enjoys shopping; the other does not. And many of you know who's who!

Her second language is Hebrew, mine Yiddish.

She likes old movies. I've never seen *Gone with the Wind*.

Sherry reads novels. I prefer nonfiction.

She's brutally honest, and I'm … a rabbi!

Sigmund Freud, who knew a little bit about marriage, suggested that it's impossible to truly know who you're marrying before you're actually wed! He believed that there are four people involved in every marriage: the woman, the man she thinks she is marrying, the man, and the woman he thinks he is marrying! Soon enough, we all learn that the person we married is not quite the person we thought they were, and at some point, many of us can't help but wonder, "What was I thinking?" It is at those moments that we would do well to remember the words of Judith Viorst: "In a grown-up marriage, we recognize that we don't always have to be in love with one another … but a grown-up marriage enables us—when we fall out of love with each other—to stick around until we fall back in."[70]

One problem is that often opposites attract—but attraction is not enough to make a partnership livable. Often the things that attracted us to our spouse are the things we come to resent! Maybe you were attracted to your spouse's dedication to their profession, and now you consider them a workaholic. You are a bit of an introvert and were attracted to your spouse's outgoing nature, and now you resent how they can't sit still for a second to listen to you! Sometimes our very physical being, which was part of the original attraction, can become a turnoff.

Question: Why are married women heavier than single women? Answer: A single woman comes home, sees what's in the refrigerator, and goes to bed. A married woman comes home, sees what's in bed, and goes to the refrigerator!

So yes, there comes a point in every marriage when our fantasies come face to face with reality. And as Perry Netter wrote in his book *Divorce Is a Mitzvah*, "This realization of the difference between fantasy and reality is the first crisis of a marriage: a crisis every married person faces."[71]

It's a crisis, however, that can be overcome, and it can help a relationship evolve in really rewarding ways. The best way I know of facing it is to recognize that when there are differences, it is not a matter of one being right and one being wrong. It's a matter of both being different—we are all different, and we all see things differently. Some of us are spenders, and some of us are savers. Some of us are quiet, and some of us are talkative. Some of us see the cup being half-full, and others see it as half-empty. That's never going to change! That's who the person has been since they were five years old! You can try to understand where your partner is coming from, and you can try to adapt. You can try to compromise. A person's behavior can be modified but not a person's nature. Trying to change the fundamental nature of your spouse is a waste of time! Remember, they might not be exactly the person you think you want now, but with patience and work and love, someday you will both come to understand how fortunate you are to have each other.

In the wonderful book *Tuesdays with Morrie*, Morrie is lying on his deathbed, and he says this:

> Say I was divorced, living alone, or had no children. This disease—what I'm going through—would be so much

harder. I'm not sure I could do it. Sure, people would come visit; friends, associates, but it's not the same as having someone who will not leave. It's not the same as having someone whom you know has an eye on you, is watching you the whole time. This is part of what a family is about, not just love, but letting others know there's someone who is watching out for them.[72]

How valuable is one human life? It's worth everything in the world if it's your spouse, your husband or wife. It's worth everything to know that someone is watching out for you—someone who will not leave! I was talking to one of the women in my congregation on the night before her husband's funeral. They had been married for half a century, and she said to me, "How am I going to manage without him? We were partners in everything we did. He put on my stockings, and I put on his socks."

I was so touched by that line—and that image of two people helping each other, taking turns, nursing each other, putting up with each other, getting each other through the travails of old age, day in and day out, year in and year out, all the years of their married life together.

The longer you live, the more you learn how much you need your spouse. At times when you can count on no one—not on friends and not even on children—your spouse will be there for you in your time of need.

Remember what Chris Rock said: "The other day I realized I've never met an elderly person that was cared for by their friends."[73]

DIVORCE

There is no such thing as an ex-wife. If you had a
relationship, just because you don't live with them anymore
doesn't mean that they're a non–human being. And if they
want to say hello, then there should be a hello.

—Willie Nelson

In November 2011, Kim Kardashian announced that she was
getting divorced. This, after seventy-two days of marriage!
This, after she had a $10 million wedding that was viewed by four
million on television! She announced it thus: "After careful consideration, I have decided to end my marriage."[74]

Careful consideration? Seventy-two days! Apparently, the an-
nouncement hadn't come as a surprise to celebrity watchers, some
of whom said they had long seen problems in the relationship.
They had "long seen problems"? Seventy-two days?

The reality is some people must come to accept that their marriage wasn't meant to be. They made a mistake—and that's no
reflection on either party. The two just couldn't face living in one
room for the rest of their lives. It is what it is! But need that be a
cause for hate? For revenge? What if I were to tell you that some

divorced couples are able to transform an unworkable marriage into a meaningful friendship. Impossible, you say?

Not to Joe DiMaggio. He was married to Marilyn Monroe for all of nine months. It must have been a stormy relationship if it couldn't last longer than that. And yet he never turned on her. He never spoke badly of her. They remained friends until her death, and afterward, he sent roses to her grave three times a week for twenty years.

You see, DiMaggio understood that some people were just not meant for each other. But even if there is no longer love, there need not be hatred. The fact that two people no longer love each other is no justification for tearing down each other or for bad-mouthing each other or pulling a Nicholas Bartha.

Nicholas Bartha and his wife, Cordula Hahn, were involved in what by any description was a bitter, bitter divorce battle. He was a native of Romania, and she was from the Netherlands. Both were highly educated people: he was a doctor, and she had a doctorate in German literature. But as smart as they were, they were not smart enough to avoid marrying the wrong person. For the final two years of their marriage, they hardly spoke to each other. The divorce battle went from court to court, with one appeal after another. Finally, in April of 2006, the New York State Supreme Court ordered Dr. Bartha to sell the town house they lived in, situated on ritzy East 62nd Street in Manhattan, in order to pay his wife what she deserved in a settlement. Four days later, New York was rocked by an explosion. Rather than sell the house and give his ex-wife her due, Dr. Bartha had blown up the house ... with himself in it![75]

An extreme case? To be sure! But I know plenty of cases where one of the spouses—or both—might have not blown up the house but still blew up the home ... bringing destruction on all involved, even their own family. Even their own children. And that's where it gets especially destructive.

The fact that two people cannot live together any longer as husband and wife does not mean that they have to blow up their family. They once loved each other. They once lived with each other. They once shared the deepest moments of intimacy, and together they bore children. The parents may be divorcing, but they have not divorced their kids. And they should not use them as pawns in their own battle—it's not their children's fault!

Sometimes, I meet with a bride and groom, and I sense tension in the room. What is it? Both sets of parents are divorced, and some have remarried. There is frustration over who is walking down the aisle—with the divorced parents, without the divorced parents, together or apart ... and what about the second husband or wife? And who is going to stand under the canopy? Suddenly the wedding aisle is being turned into a military zone! So many years later, the parents are still fighting the Wars of the Roses, making their children the monkeys in the middle, and those young, hopeful people about to embark on their own married life are being torn, tugged, and played from both sides.

And it doesn't end at the wedding! When the kids become parents, the fights center on things as meaningless as what the second spouse is going to be called. Don't do that to your kids. In this crazy, mixed-up world in which we all live, there is so much pressure and stress in a marriage. Don't add to it! If your marriage didn't work out, you must seek to understand and accept that it's not your children's fault.

We can all learn from the story of Brittany Peck's wedding. Brittany's parents had been divorced for more than a decade, and her mother had remarried. On the wedding day itself, as Brittany's biological father was walking her down the aisle, he stopped and reached out to the stepfather, asking him to join them in their walk. "He came up to me, reached out, and grabbed my hand and said, 'Hey, you've worked for this as hard as I have. You deserve this as much as I do. You're going to help me walk our daughter down the aisle. What better way to thank someone than to assist me walking our daughter down the aisle.'"

Later on, the father said, "It hasn't always been peaches and cream by any stretch of the imagination, but it looks like it was on the day it mattered most."[76]

Yes, loving and giving does not stop in divorce court. The father was right when he said that what mattered most was what happened that day. But I hope he knows that what happened on that day is going to matter for the rest of their lives.

Remember what Gwyneth Paltrow said: "I wanted to turn my divorce into a positive. What if I didn't blame the other person for anything, and held myself one hundred percent accountable? What if I checked my own s—— at the door and put my children first? And reminded myself about the things about my ex-husband that I love and fostered the friendship?"[77]

MALE AND FEMALE

When women are depressed, they either eat or go shopping.
Men invade another country. It's a whole different way of
thinking.

—Elayne Boosler

L iving in the era of gender equality, one might be tempted to be
politically correct and proclaim that male and female are the
same. They are *not*! That's what Deborah Tannen was trying to
tell us in her book *You Just Don't Understand: Women and Men in
Conversation* and what John Gray was telling us in *Men Are from
Mars, Women Are from Venus*. It's a simple fact of life: men and
women are different. The women's revolution was quite right in
proclaiming that men and women are equal in value, but let us not
make the mistake of thinking that women and men are therefore
the same. They're not.

Let me prove it to you with four vignettes found on the
internet.

One evening, a woman wrote this in her diary:

I thought he was acting weird tonight. We had made plans to meet at a bar to have a drink. I was shopping with my friends all day long, so I thought he was upset at the fact that I was a bit late, but he made no comment. Conversation wasn't flowing, so I suggested that we go somewhere quiet so we could talk. He agreed but kept quiet. I asked him what was wrong; he said nothing. I asked him if it was my fault that he was upset. He said it had nothing to do with me and not to worry.

On the way home, I told him that I loved him. He simply smiled and kept on driving. I can't explain his behavior; I don't know why he didn't say "I love you too." When we got home, I felt as if I had lost him, as if he wanted nothing to do with me anymore. He just sat there and watched a ball game on TV. He seemed distant and absent. Finally, I decided to go to bed. About ten minutes later, he came to bed, and to my surprise, he responded to my caress, and we made love, but I still felt that he was distracted. He fell asleep, and I cried. I don't know what to do. I'm sure that his thoughts are with someone else. My life is a disaster.

That same night, her husband wrote this in his diary: "Today the Yankees lost, but at least I had sex!"

Please note that this bank is installing new drive-through ATM machines, enabling customers to withdraw cash without leaving their vehicles. We ask that customers using this new facility please follow the procedures outlined below when accessing their accounts. After months of careful research, separate male and female procedures have been developed. Please follow the appropriate steps for your gender.

MALE PROCEDURE

Drive up to the cash machine.
Put down your car window.
Insert card into machine and enter PIN.
Enter amount of cash required and withdraw.
Retrieve card, cash, and receipt.
Put window up.
Drive off.

FEMALE PROCEDURE

Drive up to cash machine.
Back up the required amount to align car window with the machine.
Set parking brake, and put the window down.
Find handbag, and shake all contents onto the passenger seat to locate card.
Tell person on cell phone you will call them back, and hang up.
Attempt to insert card into machine.
Open car door to allow easier access to machine due to its excessive distance from the car.
Insert card.
Reinsert card the right way.
Dig through handbag to find diary with your PIN written on the inside back page.
Enter PIN.
Press cancel, and enter correct PIN.

Enter amount of cash required.
Check makeup in rearview mirror.
Retrieve cash and receipt.
Empty handbag again to locate wallet, and place cash inside.
Write debit amount in check register and place receipt in back
of checkbook.
Recheck makeup.
Drive forward two feet.
Reverse back to cash machine.
Retrieve card.
Reempty handbag, locate card holder, and place card into the
slot provided.
Give dirty look to irate male driver waiting behind you.
Restart stalled engine, and pull off.
Redial person on cell phone.
Drive for two to three miles.
Release parking brake.

There was a loving grandfather who always made a special effort
to spend time with his son's family on weekends. Every Sunday
morning, he would take his five-year-old granddaughter out for
a drive in the car for some quality time—pancakes, ice cream,
candy—just him and his granddaughter. One particular Sunday,
however, he had a terrible cold and could not get out of bed. He
knew his granddaughter always looked forward to their drives and
would be very disappointed. Luckily, his wife came to the rescue
and said that she would take their granddaughter for her weekly
drive and breakfast. When they returned, the little girl anxiously
ran upstairs to see her grandfather, who was still in bed.

"Well, did you enjoy your ride with Grandma?" he asked.

"Not really, Papa; it was boring. We didn't see a single pinko or Krishna schmattahead or socialist left-wing idiots or blind mamzers or Muslim terrorists anywhere we went. We just drove around, and Grandma smiled at everyone she saw. I really didn't have any fun."

The French teacher said, "In French, *house* is feminine: la maison. *Pencil* is masculine: le crayon."

One puzzled student asked, "What gender is computer?"

The teacher did not know, and the word wasn't in her French dictionary. So for fun, she split the class into two groups by gender and asked them to decide whether *computer* should be a masculine or feminine noun.

Both groups were required to give four reasons for their recommendation.

The men's group decided that computers should definitely be feminine (la computer) because:

no one but their creator understands their internal logic;
the native language they use to communicate with other computers is incomprehensible to everyone else;
even the smallest mistakes are stored in long-term memory for possible later retrieval; and
as soon as you make a commitment to one, you find yourself spending half your paycheck on accessories for it.

The women's group, however, concluded that *computer* should be masculine (le computer), because:

in order to get their attention, you have to turn them on;
they have a lot of data, but they are still clueless;
they are supposed to help you solve problems; but half the time
they *are* the problem; and
as soon as you commit to one, you realize that if you'd waited a
little longer, you could have gotten a better model.

Male and female are different, no question about it, as this passage from the medical section of the *Washington Post* explained: "Women are plagued by arthritis and bunions and bladder infections and corns and callouses and constipation and hemorrhoids and menstrual woes and migraine headaches and sleepless nights and varicose veins. In the meantime, men get heart attacks and strokes. Women are sick, but men are dead."[78]

Remember what George Carlin wrote: "Here's all you have to know about men and women: women are crazy, men are stupid. And the main reason women are crazy is that men are stupid."[79]

KNOW-IT-ALL

When I eventually met Mr. Right, I had no idea that his
first name was "Always"!

—Rita Rudner

If you search in Google for synonyms of *know-it-all*, you will find
everything from *smart aleck* to *smarty pants*, *windbag* to *wiseacre*,
cocky to *conceited*, *snotty* to *self-confident*. As Demetri Martin once
put it, "A know-it-all is a person who knows everything except for
how annoying he is."[80]

Nobody likes a know-it-all because the reality is that nobody
knows it all! And if you think you do, take this test:

How long did the Hundred Years' War last?
Which country makes Panama hats?
From which animal do we get catgut?
In what month do the Russians celebrate the October
Revolution?
What is a camel-hair brush made from?
The Canary Islands are named after which creature?
What was King George VI's first name?
What color is a purple finch?

Where are Chinese gooseberries from?
How long did the Thirty Years' War last?

Now the answers:

The Hundred Years' War lasted from 1337 to 1453 ... 116 years!
Panama hats are made in Ecuador.
Catgut comes from sheep and horses.
The October Revolution is celebrated by the Russians in November. The Russian calendar is thirteen days behind ours.
Camel-hair brushes are made from squirrel fur.
The Latin name for the Canary Islands is Insularia Canaria— Island of the Dogs.
King George VI's first name was Albert.
The color of a purple finch is crimson.
Chinese gooseberries come from New Zealand.
The Thirty Years' War lasted from 1618 to 1648 ... thirty years!

How many can get 100 percent on this exam or even a 90 or an 80 percent? The point this quiz makes is that even when things seem blindingly obvious, they are often not that simple. They serve as a quick reminder that nobody knows it all.

Indeed even if someone is incredibly good at trivia, we all are limited in our spheres of knowledge. An editor knows many things about language, logic, and grammar, but she knows next to nothing about ophthalmology. A political scientist would know how to define hegemony but might not be adept at knitting. We can all take pride in what we know.

But we should not be so overconfident and so arrogant, so cocky and so sure of ourselves and our pronouncements, because only God knows it all. The rest of us are frail, fallible human beings who often make mistakes ... even about things that we are certain we know.

For a Jew the most famous biblical commentator was a man named Rabbi Shlomo Yitzchaki, better known as Rashi. Despite the fact that he lived in the eleventh century, to this day, it's almost impossible to study the Bible or the Talmud without using Rashi's commentary. And yet in his commentary, more than a hundred times Rashi wrote, "I don't know what this means." Now Rashi didn't have to write that! He didn't have to write anything! We would never have known that his impressive understanding and knowledge did not extend to this or that verse. But without his honesty about his limitations, we never would have known how great Rashi was. His greatness is reflected not only in what he knew but in the fact that he was willing to admit what he didn't know.

You know who was also very lucky? Rashi's wife and children. Many of us are not so lucky. Many of us can testify from personal experience about a parent or teacher who was so dogmatic, so intransigent, so unwilling to allow for any discussion or give-and-take. In style and in substance, they were so smug, so certain, so authoritarian, so sure that they knew us better than we knew ourselves. And that inflexibility hurt us, frustrated us, and left us angry!

Remember, if we paid a price for the Mr. and Mrs. Know-It-Alls in our lives, we have a special responsibility to be sensitive to the fragile psyches of those who look up to us as authority figures and role models. There is a thin line separating love, caring, and concern from dominance, subjugation, and control.

Do you know anyone like that? Someone who thinks they're always right? Do you live with someone like that? You know many marriages and parent-child relationships suffer from this syndrome, and *suffer* is an apt word here. There can be no true communication, no way to resolve any disagreements. Why? Because if a person thinks he knows it all, it's hard to talk to him. If someone thinks she's always right, she might not be able to hear that she's wrong.

It's so important to listen to each other, to learn from each other. We are finite, frail, limited, and mortal human beings, and we must always recognize that little in life is certain or immutable. We dare not be know-it-alls. Coming across as one is usually a sign of weakness, not strength, bravado, or wisdom.

Remember what Malcolm Forbes said: "The dumbest people I know are those who know it all!"

HUGGING

I love hugging. I wish I was an octopus, so I could hug ten
people at a time.

—Drew Barrymore

My granddaughter spent the first year of the COVID-19 pandemic in Israel. One day, out of nowhere, she emailed her whole family: "Can't wait to come home and hug everyone!" She was not alone.

Six months into the pandemic, *Mercury News* reporter Julia Prodis Sulek asked people in the Bay Area what they were missing most. Demma Finn's answer spoke, I think, for many of us: "I am a hugger. I was born to hug people. So I have to keep my mental health in check with having to figure out different ways to connect with people. Just seeing eyes and masks really challenges you."[81]

Hugs are considered so important, and the lack of them so damaging, that in Campania, Italy, a social services consortium created a "room of hugs," an inflatable tent allowing people to hug and to touch hands in a safe way, to help those most vulnerable to COVID-19 maintain a semblance of physical contact with their loved ones.[82] Indeed, a page on the Caltech website tells us this:

Hugging is healthy: it helps the body's immune system, it keeps you healthier, it cures depression, it reduces stress, it induces sleep, it's invigorating, it's rejuvenating, it has no unpleasant side effects, and hugging is nothing less than a miracle drug.

Hugging is all natural: it is organic, naturally sweet, no pesticides, no preservatives, no artificial ingredients and 100 percent wholesome.

Hugging is practically perfect: there are no movable parts, no batteries to wear out, no periodic checkups, low energy consumption, high energy yield, inflation-proof, non-fattening, no monthly payments, no insurance requirements, theft-proof, non-taxable, non-polluting and, of course, fully returnable.[83]

As a hugger myself, I understand the therapeutic value of a hug. It helps put you in "touch" with other people.

Some years ago, a woman came into my office. She was sad and hadn't been feeling well; the years were starting to take their toll, her family lived out of town, and she was feeling all alone. We spoke for a while, and then she left. A few days later, I saw her again, and I asked her how she was doing. And she told me she had been feeling better ever since she had been in my office. I had to honestly say to her that I really didn't think I had given her any great wisdom or advice that could have made such a difference. And she said to me, "Rabbi, you don't understand. It wasn't a matter of the words you said. It was as I was leaving, the hug you gave me. It's been a long time since anyone gave me a hug. It felt so good to get one again."

Social historian and writer Ronald Blythe once said in an interview, "I think the old all need touching. They have reached the stage of life when they need kissing, hugging, and nobody touches them except the doctor." And you know what? These days, sometimes even the doctor doesn't touch you! For a fascinating look at modern surgical methods, you can't do better than a 2019 article in the *New Yorker* entitled "Paging Dr. Robot."[84]

We all know the questioning bumper sticker: "Have you hugged your kids today?" Yes, we know that kids need hugs, but we sometimes forget that grown-ups do as well. Is this not perhaps, subconsciously, one of the reasons we get married? Think back. What was the first thing you did after you were pronounced wed? So many married couples have shared that same experience. You're standing under the canopy, the officiant pronounces you married, and then what's the first thing you do? I see it all the time! There's a moment of truth, that great decision ... how are we going to kiss each other under the canopy in front of all those people? Is it going to be a modest peck on the cheek or a monster smooch? And how long should the kiss last? Every bride and groom does it their way, but every bride and groom—as soon as they are pronounced husband and wife and before that kiss—all do the same thing: they hug each other. There are times when there are no words. There are times when words aren't necessary. There are times when a hug says it all.

So listen to me, and take my words to heart: that person you hugged under the wedding canopy needs a hug just as much today as they needed it on that day—whether it was five, fifteen, or fifty years ago! Don't take it for granted. When you go home, take a good look at the person you married. Look beyond the makeup and the wrinkles, and see the woman you married, see her as she was when you fell in love with her. Look beyond the gray hair and the potbelly, and see the man you married. Really see him, with his virtues and with his faults and with his good qualities. Then give each other a hug, remembering the first one and anticipating the next one.

And don't forget: Have you hugged your kid today?

Remember what John McEnroe said: "The good part of having six kids is, there's always one who wants to hug you and say, 'Daddy, I love you.'"

PARENTING AND PERSPECTIVES

LOST CHILDHOOD

Now that I'm out of the sport, I look back and think ... I
mean, it was a gym meet—why was it so important to do
well?

—Kerri Strug

We do so much for our children, but at the same time, we
also expect so much from our children. We want only
the best for them, but then we expect the best from them, always
pushing them, filling their lives with more and more expectations.
Of course, there is nothing wrong with encouraging our children
to fulfill their potential. There is nothing wrong with encouraging our children to give their best. But there is something wrong
in expecting them to be the best. And the best in what? Is it in
character or morals? Or is it in dance and soccer? Is it in something that will make a difference to them ten years from now? We
make choices that we think someday they will come to appreciate.
But will they? Ask Kerri Strug.

Kerri Strug was the star of the 1996 Olympics. No one will
ever forget that night when Kerri combined courage with athletic
prowess to do the seemingly impossible ... to win the gold medal
in gymnastics when she was in so much pain that she could hardly

walk. During the 2004 Olympics, Eli Saslow of the *Washington Post* asked Kerri how she looked back on those moments in 1996.

Her response? "Now that I'm out of the sport, I look back and think ... I mean, it was a gym meet. Why was it so important to do well? My perspective has changed. You don't really realize how silly it all is ... it was like nothing was ever good enough. I never enjoyed the moment ... the way I perceive things now, I think it's a lot healthier. I'm just enjoying life more on a daily basis."[85]

Just eight years after winning the Olympic gold medal, Kerri Strug already saw things differently. What she had done then meant so little now. The choices she and her parents had made then would be different if she made them now. And this from a woman who won the Olympics! What of the million who don't? So ask yourselves this: Are the things you now consider important in your children's lives going to be important ten years from now?

Too often, right from birth these days, a child is put into the rat race of "making it," of being a success. There are now tutors for two- and three-year-olds to teach them how to behave and respond when "interviewed" for acceptance to prestigious pre-schools. I can't imagine what questions they ask a child at that age, except if he or she prefers cloth diapers to disposables! But those children better have the right answers, because if they don't get into the right preschool, they are not going to get into the right college. And so at the age of two or three, a baby already risks being defined as a failure and a loser.

This tremendous pressure starts with preschool and continues with afterschool activities such as soccer and piano lessons and horseback riding and enrichment classes and ice-skating. Children can be left without a minute to breathe and saddled with the fear that if they slow down, they won't have the proper credentials to get into Harvard. What a burden they now have to carry in their backpacks. Have you seen the backpacks little kids carry these days? In my mother's day, young girls had their books carried by a boy. Today, he would get a hernia! I think there must be something wrong when I go into Toys"R"Us to buy a present for a grandchild, and I see iPads intended for children. So young and already so programmed! Whatever happened to those words: "Just go outside and play!"

And their play now is in structured Little Leagues where the children's competition on the field is heightened and exacerbated by the parents' competition off the field. They even have a name for it now! It's called *sideline rage*, with parents yelling and jeering and fighting at their kids' athletic games. All so that their kids can be winners!

It's no way for children to live—with a constant consciousness of grades and rank and status, of the need to win and achieve, to care so much about the difference between a 3.5 and a 3.9 GPA, to move from IQ to SAT, from preschool to high school to college to graduate school on a treadmill, to know that the meaning of their lives (and their parents' lives) hangs on grades and admissions and trophies. But it's the way too many of our children are living these days. And for what? For their success? Or is it for ours?

There used to be a popular comedian on the borscht belt named Emil Cohen. In his comic routine, he used to speak of his two young sons as "One's a doctor, the other a lawyer. The doctor is six, and the lawyer is three." The line was cute, but it can also be dangerous.

Our children are not *nachas* (pride) producing machines. Not every child can become a doctor or lawyer. Some are going to have to settle for the rabbinate! We lie to ourselves in thinking that we can decide who and what our children are going to become. Right from the beginning, the cord must be cut. Yes, every parent should want their child to become a healthy, decent, mature human being. But at some point, we all have to accept the fact that our children may not turn out to be exactly who and what we want them to be. They are going to make decisions for themselves. Yes, we have to try and teach them to make the right decisions ... but they are the ones who are going to have to decide what decision is right for them. At some point, with our children we can recommend and suggest, but we cannot impose. We cannot possess.

Remember what George Clooney said: "My parents were disappointed I didn't finish college, and they were really upset when I went to Hollywood to become an actor. I was a big disappointment to them."

PERFECTION

Me having a beautiful wife and great family around me, all the money I've got, all the things that I've got, a Ferrari that I just ripped the top off and turned into a convertible, the rings I got, the two mansions on the water, a master's in criminal justice, I'm a cop, plus I look good. So me shooting 40 percent at the foul line is just God's way of saying that nobody's perfect. If I shot 90 percent from the line, it just wouldn't be right.

—Shaquille O'Neal

The Jewish people start their New Year by wishing each other a *Shana Tova*—a good year. Why just *good*? Why not *great, terrific,* or *perfect*? I guess we are being realistic right from the start of the year because rarely are things great, terrific, or perfect. And good is good enough!

In 2018, journalist Maggie Parker wrote an article entitled "The Irrational Desire Driving Millennials and Gen Z into Depression."[86] And what is that irrational desire? The article tells us, "Kids these days are more obsessed with perfection than many previous generations were, and this obsession is associated with increased depression and anxiety."

You and I know that it's not just kids!

Many of us are living in nicer homes than our parents ever had. Many of us are making more money than we ever dreamed of. And yet so many of us are unhappy because we think the person next door or down the street has more. We always think that! We always think that our neighbor's wife is better put together, our neighbor's husband makes more money, our neighbor's children are more successful, our neighbor's parents more understanding. We always think that they—those lucky neighbors—have it all.

But nobody has it all. God so often seems to give with one hand and withhold with the other. The one who has a good business, alas, may have bad health. The one who has good health may have delinquent children. The one who has good children may have a business that is on the edge of bankruptcy. We've got to learn this about ourselves and about others. We can't have it all. I met someone who had been fixed up on a date with a lovely, talented, successful woman. Afterward, I asked him what he thought. He said, "She's nice, but she doesn't like camping, and I do, so I'm not going to call her again." I thought he was making a big mistake. His big mistake was not looking in the mirror and discovering that there's a shortage of perfect people in this world. You should not require nor desire perfection, not from others and not from yourself. Because if you do, you are bound to be disappointed. No one has it all.

Maureen Dowd, who usually comments—in a rather acerbic manner—on the political world, once wrote a column that was rather mellow and quite different for her. It was entitled "An Ideal Husband."[87] In light of the headlines being made at that time by the failure of several celebrity marriages (such as Christie Brinkley and Peter Cook), Maureen Dowd got in touch with Father Pat Connor, a seventy-nine-year-old Catholic priest from Bordentown, New Jersey, who had been going around for forty years giving a lecture called "Whom Not to Marry." She asked him to summarize his talk (and I am paraphrasing it further for clarity):

Do not marry someone who has no friends.
What are their friends like?
What do your friends and family members think of your intended?
Is your intended responsible with money? Stingy?
Avoid marrying a doormat, someone whose life you can run.
Don't marry someone believing you can change them.
Does this person have a sense of humor? Clingy parents? Do they come from a family that seems racist or sexist?
Do you have common goals, and are your values aligned?
Is your intended ready to forgive, praise, and be polite? Or are they easily angered, controlling, secretive, envious, or given to lying?

I thought that was a pretty good list ... despite the fact that I'm the only person I could think of who meets all of its qualifications! But there were many people who disagreed with the list, and several even wrote letters to the *New York Times* saying that they had a better list! One of those was a woman named Susan Striker, and here is what she had to say:

To the Editor:

I am a twice-divorced woman and after my second divorce I sat down and wrote a message to women, including these words of advice:
Never marry a man who yells at you in front of his friends.
Never marry a man who is more affectionate in public than in private.

Never marry a man who notices all of your faults, but never notices his own.

Never marry a man whose first wife had to sue him for child support.

Never marry a man who corrects you in public.

Never marry a man who sends birthday cards to his ex-girlfriends.

Never marry a man who doesn't treat his dog nicely.

Never marry a man who is rude to waiters.

Never marry a man who doesn't love music.

Never marry a man whose plants are all dead.[88]

You tell me: Is it any wonder that Susan Striker has been divorced twice? Is there any man who could please her?

I know a lot of people who do much worse than let their plants die. Some of them don't hang up their clothes—real slobs! Some of them can't boil an egg. Some of them would throw up if they changed a diaper! Some don't like being interrupted when they're watching a football game on TV. Some have potbellies. Some ... well, you know what they do with the toilet seat! So no, there are no perfect men, and there are no perfect women, which means there is no perfect wife or husband.

It would be bad enough if we were demanding only perfection from our partners, parents, friends, or children. However, more and more people are less and less satisfied with themselves. An image of perfection has been created for us, and we despair when we fail to achieve the perfect image. One must be bright, witty, upbeat, and good looking; one's pants must fit just right; one must have no flab around the waist, have a great salary, and be a good tennis player, skier, swimmer—your plain, simple, ordinary, everyday six-million-dollar bionic human. There is a whole cult of perfection foisted upon us, and it's dragging us down emotionally. That's what prompted Mildred Newman to write her book *How to Be Your Own Best Friend*.[89] In it, she challenges us to learn how to accept our imperfections, to live with and appreciate ourselves. This is crucial because if we cannot live with ourselves, who could possibly stand to live with us?

It seems to me that frequently in modern American society, the issue is no longer "keeping up with the Joneses" or "keeping up with the Rockefellers." Today it's keeping up with our glorified fantasies. Of course, these fantasies have always existed, but there used to be a time when we realized that they were only to be found in Hollywood or on Broadway. But now, wherever we go, we see books on the perfect *this* or the perfect *that*, and we have started believing it all. We have started to expect and accept only perfection in our lives.

Don't misunderstand me. I am certainly not advocating half-hearted efforts, settling for the easy way out, simply getting by, or never striving for higher and higher goals. What I am saying is that frequently today we are, tragically, our own worst critics. Sorry, none of us are perfect! And even if there were such a thing as a perfect husband or wife, would they have married us?

You can't have it all. Good is good enough! And you are good enough.

Remember what the Rolling Stones sang: "You can't always get what you want, but if you try sometimes, you just might find you get what you need."

PARENTS

If I'm more of an influence to your son as a rapper than
you are as a father ... you got to look at yourself as a parent.
—Ice Cube (born O'Shea Jackson)

The popular 1991 movie *City Slickers* describes the lives of three men, all around the age of forty and all about to confront a midlife crisis. In one poignant scene, the three men get into a discussion about what had been the best day of their lives.

For one, that day was when he was seven years old and his father took him to his first baseball game at Yankee Stadium. He remembered walking through a dark tunnel but feeling secure because his father was holding his hand ... and then they came into the light, and there before him unfolded the green of the baseball field. It was the first time he had watched a baseball game in full color, and it was on that day that Mickey Mantle hit a home run, and his father taught him how to keep score. That, for him, was the best day of his life.

For our second grumpy old man, it was his wedding day. He remembers his friends sitting there smiling, and as he walked down the aisle, his father, who was an unaffectionate man, gave him a wink. It was at that moment he finally felt grown up ... the best day of his life.

The third one chooses a very different kind of day as the best day of his life. It was when he was a teenager and his mother and father were fighting again. His father had once again been caught being unfaithful, and while his parents were screaming at each other, he came in and told his father to get out, that he would take care of the house. And his father left. That, he says, was the best day of his life. Then he adds, "It was also the worst day of my life."

Three very different kinds of days with three very different settings: a baseball park, a wedding, a family separation. But all three have one common denominator. They involved something that parents did while completely unaware that their children were watching and recording it all. Holding the child's hand, teaching him how to keep score, a wink of approval—all of these are small, seemingly insignificant gestures, so different from a major family upheaval, and yet these all have a profound impact years later in ways we can never imagine because our children were watching and recording.

The best day of their lives ... the worst day of their lives ... we are the ones who make it happen. And unfortunately, all too often, we don't even know it.

Charles Francis Adams served for many years as ambassador from the United States to Great Britain. He was busy with affairs of state and evidently did not have too much time to give his family. His son Brooks Adams and he had very interesting notes in their diaries about a day they'd spent together fishing.

His son wrote the following entry: "Went fishing with my father. The most glorious day in my life."

The father had this entry in his diary about the very same day: "Went fishing with my son. A day wasted." The father didn't realize the impact he was having on his child.

Bob Alper, a professional rabbi and comedian, wrote a touching piece on "The Glance."

It was a hot Friday afternoon in June 1980. The academic year was drawing to an end, and it was time for the Jarrettown Elementary School's annual musical extravaganza:

The day's piece de resistance was the chorus. Fifty-seven magnificently gifted, musically accomplished children of grades three through five filed onto the stage with a minimum of fuss and murmuring, took their places, and faced the conductor sitting at her piano. On the left side of the second row, three kids from the end, wearing a formerly all-white and now slightly spotted shirt, stood Zack Alper. Age eight.

Fridays were busy days at my synagogue. That morning, I tried to work a little faster, tried to attend to as many details as possible. Over breakfast, Zack assured his mother and me that we really didn't need to come to the concert. "I'm just in the chorus. I'm not doing a solo or anything." "Well," we told him, "let's see how the day goes." We both had every intention of attending, and we did.

As for the audience, all eyes focused on one kid and one kid only: their own. Sherri and I watched Zack, of course, knowing that he was uncertain as to whether we'd be there. The conductor raised her baton and tapped for attention. Seventy-one percent of the choristers actually faced her, and nearly all of them hit the first note, some a little sooner than others. And—we were off.

We were proud, of course. Zack seemed to be singing all the words and paying some attention to the music. Even though we sat toward the rear of the large room, I could see that he was actually focusing on the teacher every once in a while. But most of the time his eyes were darting about, looking quickly in one direction, then another. Searching.

Then he spotted us. Just a split second. The briefest of moments. He spotted us, and there it was: "the glance." That wonderful look, that extraordinary connection when a child discovers his parents. Zack didn't stop singing, but we could see an almost imperceptible grin start and then stop just as quickly. His eyes rolled slightly upward in a similarly happy grimace, a "yeah, I knew you'd be here" kind of expression. Then it was over.

"The glance." A split second. The tiniest fragment of a life. And it was worth everything, everything just to be part of it.

Later, Zack accepted our words of praise with the modesty of a professional. Finally, he offered, "You didn't have to come. I was only in the chorus. I've gotta take the chairs back to Miss Gradwell's room now." But the good-bye hug and kiss we each received was more than his typical afternoon quickie.

All of us who are parents should ask ourselves how often we pause to realize that we are daily making indelible entries into our children's books of life. We need to grow more aware of how enduring these influences will prove to be. The amount of charity we give, the excuses we offer for not giving, the comments we make behind the backs of friends, the references we make to the color of a person's skin, our business ethics, our moral behavior, how we act at parties, what we eat and drink and watch on television … all these and so much more are being inscribed into the temple walls of our children's minds and are being videotaped on the camcorder of their souls.

Just ask Tim Russert. The late television personality Tim Russert had great respect for his father, and he even wrote a book about him. In that book, he tells a story about how his father once took him to a ball game. He bought tickets for them way up in the bleachers because that was all his father could afford. They went to the stadium, and they were climbing up the stairs toward the bleachers when a group of kids broke down the barrier between the high-priced seats and the low-priced seats. The kids went piling into the high-priced section, and Tim said to his father, "C'mon, let's go with them."

But his father pulled him back and said just one thing. He said, "No way. Our seats are up there."[90] Forty years later, Tim Russert remembered that story. That was the way his father taught him to live. That was the way his father taught him to be ethical and play by the rules. And he never got over that single sentence, "Our seats are up there."

Is that the way you want to be remembered?

Remember what Garrison Keillor wrote: "Nothing you do for your children is ever wasted. They seem not to notice us, hovering, averting our eyes and they seldom offer thanks, but what we do for them is never wasted."[91]

ENTITLEMENT

There's no such thing as an entitlement, unless someone
has first met an obligation.

—Margaret Thatcher

Originally the word *entitled* referred to someone who had a
title—that is, a rank or office. Now, many a common man
believes himself to be "entitled." For example, from 2016 through
2020, common man Jared Kushner was one of the most powerful
people in America. As son-in-law and advisor to the president, he
had input on most every decision affecting our country—indeed,
our world.

Peter Beinart, writing in the *Forward*, challenged us to look
at how Kushner came to power and to contrast that to how other
Jews before him came to power.[92] Louis Brandeis, Alan Greenspan,
Ruth Bader Ginsburg, Lawrence Summers, Walter Rostow, Henry
Kissinger ... just about every one of them came to power on merit.
They were successful as lawyers, businesspeople, and academicians
who rose to the top as a result of their own efforts and talents. Jared
Kushner? He was born into extreme wealth and was no great stu-
dent in high school. It is reported he got into Harvard after his
father made a $2 million contribution. With the family real estate

money, he bought a newspaper, invested in a major property in New York for which he overpaid, and is now having difficulty meeting mortgage payments. Because of this, the US Office of Government Ethics reported that "officials from four countries have discussed ways they could use Kushner's intricate business arrangements, lack of experience, and financial woes to manipulate him."[93]

Jared Kushner got where he is today based not on merit but on money, not on sterling character but on social class. What prepared him for such a position of power at the right hand of the most powerful person on earth? In the words of the *Economist* magazine, "Kushner's self-possession now seems anchored more in a feeling of entitlement than steadfastness."[94]

Kushner is not alone! Few were shocked by this March 12, 2019, *New York Times* headline: "Actresses, Business Leaders, and Other Wealthy Parents Charged in US College Entry Fraud."[95] Fifty people in six states were accused by the Justice Department of taking part in a major college-admission scandal. They included Hollywood actresses, business leaders, and elite college coaches.

A day later, writing in the *Wall Street Journal*, Jason Gay said it all: "There is something so entitled and 2019 about all of it—yet another example of the powerful endorsing cheating and lying, and rationalizing that the scammery doesn't really matter, if the ends justify the means. Hard work, integrity, truth ... those are increasingly quaint values to an entitlement culture conditioned to get what it wants and believe what it wants to believe."[96]

Of course, all children start off with a sense of entitlement, a sense of knowing it all, a desire for instant gratification. But rather than helping them outgrow it, these days more and more of us are instead continuing to feed that sense as our children get older. Jennifer Senior, in her book *All Joy and No Fun: The Paradox of Modern Parenthood*, wrote, "The author observes the shift now that children are not a source of labor for the family, that they have gone from employees of the parents to the bosses of the parents."[97]

Several years ago, I read something in a blog (something that I can no longer find) that I jotted down because it spoke to my concern about children:

> I have worked the last six years in higher education, and with each passing year, the students I work with come in expecting more and more, wanting fast, efficient service, wanting all of their desires taken care of, wanting close and convenient parking for their car, wanting a large suite-style apartment to hold all their belongings, wanting to easily pass their classes. And the kicker for all of this is that in the "market" for students, to keep enrollment high, higher education institutions have catered to this! They continue to provide all these conveniences to students. If our educational system continues to bend over backward for students' "needs" in order to keep them enrolled in their particular school, then how are we really educating our next generation? What is their fate? What is our fate? What is the fate of the world?
>
> I see a manifestation of this sense of entitlement every summer now. It used to be when you asked kids what they planned to do during the summer, you got the response that they were either going to camp or looking for a job. You can't assume that's the answer anymore. During the summer, I spend time in Ocean City, and most of the kids I come across working there are from Latvia or Ukraine or Bulgaria. Too many kids aren't working during the summer anymore. You know why? Because they are in Majorca or Cancun. You can't expect them to work during

the summer … they need a vacation! After all, they went to school all year! Take note at any airport: teenagers are already experienced world travelers. Listen to some of their conversations: "You mean you've never been to Jamaica?" or "This is only your second trip to Israel?"

I would remind them of the words of Abraham Lincoln: "You have to do your own growing no matter how tall your grandfather was." Those who preceded us were part of what has been called the greatest generation. Greatness cannot be an inheritance. It must be an achievement.

Before we lay this all at the feet of our children, let's remember that many of us adults suffer from this syndrome as well. Israelis express it in the two Hebrew words *magiya li*, but as a child, I learned it as three Yiddish words, *es kumt mir*, which means "I am entitled" or "It's coming to me."

David Brooks wrote a wonderful op-ed column in the *New York Times* entitled "The Great Seduction," in which he pointed out, "Between 1989 and 2001, credit-card debt nearly tripled, soaring from $238 billion to $692 billion. By last year [2007], it was up to $937 billion."[98] That's not debt from college students—we put ourselves into debt. Why? Because we are entitled! If our next door neighbor has it, why shouldn't we? We are just as good! We are just as deserving! We work just as hard!

Think about it! Do you know people who are like that? And if you really think about it, you might realize that you're one of them, the kind of person who says, "I'm entitled to a three-car garage just like my friend across the street. He has it only because his father is wealthy, but I'm just as entitled."

Or maybe you're like the person who thinks, "What's she got that I ain't got? She only looks that good because of the clothing she buys. I'm entitled to it just as much as she is. I work hard while she just sits at home."

Or maybe you're like the parents who drive up to school in a Lexus and apply for financial assistance: "After all, we've got a reputation to live up to, and if others are paying just this much, why shouldn't we?"

Remember what Marian Wright Edelman said: "Don't feel entitled to anything you didn't sweat and struggle for."[99]

Sibling Rivalry

Siblings: children of the same parents, each of whom is perfectly normal until they get together.

—Sam Levenson

All our parents had different hopes, dreams, and expectations for us. But I think all of them shared one hope in common: they wanted us to get along with our brothers and sisters. And I know that's not always easy to do. So much of who and what we are is a result of who our siblings are. In our most formative years, we spend more time with our siblings than with friends, parents, and teachers or even by ourselves. But somewhere down the line, something shifts. We discover that despite our shared genetics, environment, and experiences, are not the same. And we don't like the differences we perceive. But you know what? As brothers and sisters, we don't have to like everything about each other in order to love each other.

Look at the relationship between Shirley MacLaine and Warren Beatty. They see eye to eye on very little, and yet they have a very deep relationship. When Shirley MacLaine was asked to explain it, she replied in two words: "We're blood." I love that! "We're blood." It's as simple as that.

We can't change who and what our siblings are. But as we get older, our relationship with our siblings can change. In our mobile society, where the concept of *lifelong friends* is hard to sustain, it is our siblings we can turn to in times of need. It is our siblings who are going to mourn for us. And it is our siblings with whom we will mourn.

I recently read a book entitled *Fathers Aren't Supposed to Die* by T. M. Shine. It's the story of five brothers who have grown distant in life when suddenly they all get the phone call, the phone call all of us must inevitably get. Their father is lying in a hospital bed unable to speak, bleeding in the brain. The book poignantly describes how each of the brothers deals with their father's death, but more so, it describes how the brothers now deal with each other. A few sentences on the last page tell it all. The author wrote the following:

> I think about how those days I spent holed up in the hospital rooms with my brother Will were like when we brothers were jammed into a small bedroom as kids. I find some solace that we were so close in the beginning and so close in the end. Like so many fractured relationships, maybe those are the only times that really matter. Maybe. But my heart truly tells me that it's in the middle that we need one another the most. That is the only thing I have learned from this ordeal. It is my regret.[100]

Yes, at the beginning and end, brothers and sisters are together. But if you're not together now, reach out, because it's in the middle when you need each other the most.

There's one thing more. When brothers and sisters fight, when husbands and wives argue, and most certainly when children and parents quarrel, the least important question is who's right. That question takes you nowhere. The real question is this: How do you stay together? Sure, Daddy shouldn't have remarried so quickly ... but so what? Sure, Ellen shouldn't have moved to California ... but so what? Sure, Mom shouldn't have tried to tell me what to do with my life ... but so what? Sure, Freddie shouldn't have invested in a fly-by-night scheme that I warned him about ... but so what? Who cares who was right? What does it matter who should have done what yesterday? How will answering those questions preserve the relationship? How will being right keep you from losing someone you love?

The only thing that counts today is preventing distance from setting in, because distance begets distance, silence begets silence, and separation begets separation. Forgetting leaves us all forgotten.

I know of a man who lived a long full life. He wasn't very wealthy, but he left three successful sons. And in his will, he divided his estate equally among the three of them. But he put a certain amount of money aside for them to use in a specific way. This was what he wrote in his will: "Every year on the anniversary of my death, if you will come to synagogue and say kaddish for me ... that would be nice. If you give charity in my memory ... that would be okay. But what would be most important for me is if every year on that day, you use some of this money for the three of you to get together to go out for lunch. Knowing that you are together would be the greatest honor you can ever pay me."

"We're blood." It's as simple as that!

Remember what Dylan Thomas wrote: "It snowed last year too: I made a snowman and my brother knocked it down and I knocked my brother down and then we had tea."[101]

JUDGING

I can't go anywhere without someone judging me.

—Britney Spears

B ritney Spears strove for attention, but she paid a bitter price for it! That sense of constantly being seen and judged and found wanting is hard to endure. However, the truth of the matter is it is not just the rich and famous who are constantly being placed under the microscope. It's all of us! All of us get judged by others; indeed, all of us judge others.

The People's Court is not restricted to our TV screens. The people's court takes place every time friends get together for a dinner party and sit around talking. And what do they talk about? They talk about others:

Did you hear about Phil? He was just laid off again—a real loser.

I wonder why Sam's family put him in a nursing home. They have enough money for twenty-four-hour home care.

Did you hear about Frank and Sandy? They are separating. I knew it ... they never should have gotten married!

Did you hear about the Smith kid? A real pothead ... dropping out of college. It is the parents' fault—they were always going on vacation.

I could add to the list—and so could you! And so many *do*, never thinking to give the people involved the benefit of the doubt, never knowing what is really going on behind closed doors.

I was once interviewed by *Baltimore* magazine, and they asked if a movie were made of my life, who I would like to star as me. The first words that came out of my mouth were "Chris Rock." I said that not just because we bear such a close resemblance but because I love his funny, affable, irreverent nature. Then I read an article about Chris Rock. That funny, outgoing guy on stage? When he steps off the stage, he is a painfully shy human being, extremely uncomfortable around others. Who would have known?

Or try this one. One of the greatest basketball players of all time was Bill Russell, who led the Boston Celtics to numerous world championships. He is considered the best defensive center ever. Because he was six feet eleven, and had a scowling face, other players were afraid to go up against him. But in his biography, Mr. Russell revealed that before every game, he used to throw up because he was so nervous about playing. Who would have known?

If you knew how hard that man who has trouble holding down a job works to be able to make it, maybe you would give him the benefit of the doubt and offer not judgment but compassion. If you knew how hard the couple worked to try and make their marriage last or how much pain and turmoil parents go through with a troubled child ... if you had any idea how they really felt, maybe you would give them the benefit of the doubt.

Don't be so quick to judge! When people say something stupid or hurtful or incendiary—when friends or relatives exhibit insensitivity and thoughtlessness—try not to take it personally. You don't know what they are going through! That's life! What people say and do in one set of circumstances are often things they might not say or do under different circumstances.

The sages in the Talmud teach this: "Do not judge your friend until you stand in their shoes." Well, let me tell you what I think our sages really meant by that. Our sages meant that you can never judge anyone because you can never fully stand in someone else's shoes!

No, we can't ever really know where another is coming from. And yet we have to try. After all, we would like others to be sensitive to our circumstances. We would like others, before judging us, to try and understand where we are coming from. Just think how much better off we would be—how generation gaps could be bridged—if we strove to put ourselves in other people's shoes as best we could.

What if parents and children who are divided by a generation gap were to switch roles in their imagination and put themselves into each other's shoes. We judge our children! We do it all the time! We say that they are unappreciative, think everything is coming to them, don't call often enough, or don't give us much time. And they are certainly making all sorts of mistakes in the way they are raising their children. All this might be true, but think of it from their perspective: their insecurities, their being caught up in a society where the challenge is not to make a buck but to make a million bucks, their fears about keeping up, and their own inner struggles and questions about how to do right by their kids and their spouses, with all the pressures that are on them. Their experiences—the things that shape and form them—are different from the experiences that shaped and formed us. And so if we want to understand our children, we have to somehow, hard as it may be, try to climb out of ourselves and imagine ourselves in their situation. If we do, then we'll understand them more and judge them less.

And they have to do the same thing if they are to understand us—their parents. They judge us frequently. They lose patience with us when we seem to repeat ourselves too often, are a little edgier around small children then we used to be, or are a bit more demanding of attention. What they have to do if they want to understand us is climb up out of themselves and imagine themselves through time and space into our situation and what it feels like knowing that you're getting older and you're not able to do what you used to do. They have to imagine what it feels like when life-long friends are dying or having life-threatening operations and you can't help but wonder when it's going to be your turn. They have to know that even though we're at a stage in life where we've "made it," that doesn't mean we don't have some very real needs! If our children could feel what we feel, they would understand what makes us tick, what makes us act and think the way we do.

So we all have this challenge. I know that it's hard—terribly hard—to see the world from someone else's point of view, and yet that is precisely what we must try to do, as best as we can, if we are to bring about change and reconciliation in our collective and personal lives.

And even if it proves impossible to put ourselves in another's shoes, just knowing and understanding our inability to do that may stop us from being so quick to judge.

Remember what Mel Brooks said: "Tragedy is when I cut my finger. Comedy is when you fall into an open sewer and die."

GROWING UP AND GROWING OLD

OLD AGE

Old age isn't a battle; old age is a massacre.

—Philip Roth

Hunter S. Thompson was a well-known US journalist and author. He wrote articles and novels, including *Fear and Loathing in Las Vegas*, in a style that became known as *gonzo journalism*. He must have had an interesting life, because he is quoted as having said, "I hate to advocate drugs, alcohol, violence, or insanity to anyone, but they've always worked for me." And yet on February 20, 2005, he took his life while sitting in the kitchen of his home near Aspen, Colorado. He took his life while his son, daughter-in-law, and grandson were playing in the next room. He took his life while talking to his wife on the phone.

As bad as *how* he took his life was *why* he took his life. He chose to kill himself—at the ripe old age of sixty-seven—rather than face "the indignities of old age."[102] Yes, growing old requires sacrifices, and some people are just not prepared to make them.

The truth of the matter is there are many indignities that come with old age. It is a time of aches and pains and doctor visits. It is a time that can bring catheters and incontinence and surgery and respirators, a time of fear of falls and pneumonia and Parkinson's and Alzheimer's. I know a man confined to a wheelchair, dependent on his wife and an aide to dress him and feed him and bathe him and wipe off the food that dribbles from the side of his mouth. The stroke made him an invalid. I am told that his mind is still good. And so I look at him and think to myself, "What's going on in his mind? What is he thinking?" This man was part of what has been dubbed the greatest generation. He had the strength to live through the Depression, the courage to fight overseas in World War I. This man built a successful company. He called all the shots; he was in control. And now? Now, what does he know? He knows the indignities of old age. And he is not alone.

Even if we are spared these particular indignities, there are others that come with our growing older. As we get older, we have to face the reality that we ain't what we used to be! And even if we are, people still think we ain't! Little wonder that Dr. Zeke Emanuel, one of our country's most respected bioethicists, once wrote an article for *The Atlantic* titled, "Why I Hope to Die at 75."[103] The article made the argument that those who live past seventy-five are no longer really productive members of society. They become a burden on our country's health resources, and living longer is going to only make matters worse. In Emanuel's own words, "Here is a simple truth that many of us seem to resist: living too long is also a loss. It robs us of our creativity and ability to contribute to work, society, and the world. We are no longer remembered as vibrant and engaged but as feeble, ineffectual, even pathetic."

So there it is. After a 3,300-year-old biblical mandate—"And thou shall choose life"—Zeke Emanuel and many others like him are choosing death instead ... as if after seventy-five, there is not much you can do, so you may as well roll over and die.

Not me! And I hope not you! I learned this from people much smarter than Zeke Emanuel:

I think of Dylan Thomas's great poem where he tells his suffering father, "Do not go gentle into that good night. / Rage, rage against the dying of the light."[104] Don't die, Dad, while you're still alive.

I think of Moses. If ever there were a man who should have been prepared to accept death, it was him! He knew the glories that would await him in the afterlife. He fulfilled the dream we traditionally express: "You should live until 120 years." We say that because Moses did live that long! And yet when it came time for him to die, the Midrash tells us that Moses cried out to God: "If I can't live as a human, let me live as an animal who can still live and experience this world."

I think of the powerful words of the poet, songwriter, and entertainer Leonard Cohen, in his haunting song "Dance Me to the End of Love," which begins with the verse, "Dance me to your beauty with a burning violin." He explained that the song was inspired by the Holocaust, and the burning violin referred to the music that Jewish prisoners were forced to play as string quartets in the Nazi extermination camps moments before they were to be put to death. They had one last chance to create beautiful music, and so they played their hearts out "with a burning violin." The Nazis might have chosen death, but countless others have always chosen life right up until the end.

That acceptance is not always easy to achieve. I can understand why. Philip Roth spoke for many when he wrote, "Old age isn't a battle; old age is a massacre."[105]

The Bible is sensitive to all this. It is reflected in the job that God assigned to the first Levites. They were the ones who did all the work in the tabernacle; they lifted and dismantled and unloaded and put together again all the furniture in the sanctuary. The Bible tells us that they were eligible to start performing their tasks when they turned thirty. But then we are told that the Levites performed their jobs until they were fifty, and that was it. It was time to retire. They couldn't do this job anymore.

But that's not the end of the story! After the Levites stopped doing all the physical work in the tabernacle, when they could no longer carry the heavy pieces of furniture, you know what they did? They sang in the temple choir! You can't teach an old dog new tricks? Sure you can!

This is what we mean when we give the traditional greeting, "May you go from strength to strength." When you no longer have the strength to do what you've been doing, may you find the strength to do other things with your life.

Remember the words inscribed on a stone covering the ashes of Malcolm Forbes: "While alive, he lived."[106]

Good Old Days

"Kids are different today," I hear every mother say ...
　　　—The Rolling Stones, "Mother's Little Helper"

People seem to have a tendency to picture the past as a magical time, something much better than it really was. Whatever is wrong today, they think things were much better in "the good old days," somehow blurring the reality that the good old days weren't really that good. It is this syndrome that perhaps gave rise to the famous song lyric "Those were the days, my friends. We thought they'd never end." It's a great song ... but it's dangerous! It reinforces the misconception that now we've got problems, but back then? Those were the days, my friends.

If that's what you think, let me tell you something about the good old days. Read these words:

There is yet one other evil disease regarding raising children that is not practiced by other peoples. A child sits at the table with his father and mother, and he is the first to stretch forth his hand to partake of the food. He thus grows up arrogant, without fear or culture or refinement, acting as if his father and mother were his friends or siblings. By the time he is eight or nine years old and his parents wish to correct their earlier mistakes, they no longer are able to, for childish habit has already become second nature …

Another bad and bitter practice: parents take a child to school and, in front of the child, warn the teacher not to punish him. When the child hears this, he no longer pays attention to his schoolwork and his disobedience grows worse. This was not the practice of our ancestors. In their days, if a child came crying to his father and mother and told of being punished by a teacher, they would send with him a gift to the teacher, and congratulate the teacher.

This report comes to us from Rabbi Moshe Hagiz, and it was written over 250 years ago! Those were the days, my friends. Today's version can be found in any bookstore with titles like *Overindulged Children*, *Spoiling Childhood*, *The Myth of Self-Esteem*, *The Pampered Child Syndrome*, *The Omnipotent Child*, *Generation Me*, and *The Narcissism Epidemic*. Many a parent shares the sentiment of Lillian Carter, Jimmy Carter's mother, who once said, "When I look at my children, I say, 'Lillian, you should have stayed a virgin.'"[107]

We make a big mistake when we depict today's children as somehow less than the children of previous generations, as if they're all potential "Columbine murderers"—undisciplined, unrestrained, immoral, and spoiled. Need I remind you that in the good old days, Cain killed Abel, Esau tried to kill Jacob, and Joseph's brothers made a similar attempt. Those were the days, my friends.

Kids today are no better or worse than before. They are all what kids have always been: bearers of unlimited potential, with a natural striving for the good and the holy. To think of them as being anything else, to think that things used to be better, robs the present and the future of much joy and happiness.

I thought about this recently when I read an article about the Lower East Side of New York. The whole area is undergoing an urban renewal—there are tours showing some of what's left of the good old days that we Jews so nostalgically recall about the Lower East Side. You speak of the Lower East Side, and the images that immediately come to mind seem like a golden age for the Jewish people: Yiddish theatres and synagogues and knishes and pushcarts and "Bei Mir Bistu Shein" and children running in the streets and families celebrating together. Maybe those were the days, my friends.

But let me let you in on a little secret: it wasn't quite like that. There is a wonderful book called *A Bintel Brief: Sixty Years of Letters from the Lower East Side to the Jewish Daily Forward*.[108] The *Jewish Daily Forward* was the newspaper for the Jews on the Lower East Side at the turn of the last century, and A Bintel Brief was one of its most popular columns. It was our people's version of Dear Abby, with people writing in and asking advice in regard to all areas of their lives. Read those letters, and you will get a clearer picture of the good old days.

There are letters written about poverty and unemployment and starvation, about young people in the sweatshops developing tuberculosis, about young girls lured into brothels. Many are pathetic, touching letters from despairing women whose husbands had deserted them and their children, leaving them with no means of support. Those were the days, my friends. The number of men who left their families grew so great at one point that the *Forward*, with the help of the National Desertion Bureau, established a special column to trace them. So much for the good old days.

Brooks Atkinson, a famous theater critic for the *New York Times*, was right on the mark when he wrote, "In every age the 'good old days' were a myth. No one ever thought they were good at the time, for every age has consisted of crises that seemed intolerable to the people who lived through them."[109]

Remember what Tom Clancy wrote: "The good old days are now!"

SATISFIED

Having it all is the worst. No matter how much we all have and how grateful we are for what we have, no one has it all because we all make tradeoffs every single day, every single moment.

—Sheryl Sandberg, COO of Facebook

I once read something Martha Stewart apparently said in an interview, and it stuck with me: "I have a beautiful weekend house in the Hamptons, but it is not, as it turns out, my summer dream house. It doesn't have the view of the ocean that I absolutely want, it doesn't have the rustic wood floors that I absolutely crave, it doesn't have a little dock to which I can tie my little rowboat, and it doesn't have the shallow water of a quiet lagoon where I can pick my plants."

These words go a long way toward explaining Martha Stewart's 2001 downfall. Here was a woman who had come to personify good taste, proper etiquette, and gracious living. This woman had everything: fame, admiration, money—lots of money. On the day the jury gave its verdict in her insider-trading trial, Martha Stewart was worth an estimated $420 million! But somehow, that wasn't enough to satisfy her. To save $50,000, she was ready to take a risk that put her in the slammer. Maybe she thought the extra money would give her the "rustic wood floors" that she "absolutely craved." Or the view of the ocean that she "absolutely wanted." How could she settle for less?

If, like Martha Stewart, you always want it all, nothing will ever be good enough, and you'll never make your peace with anything! You'll be like Leona Helmsley, the real estate mogul, replete with fame and fortune, who sued Woodlawn Cemetery in the Bronx for $150 million before disinterring and relocating the body of her third husband, Harry. Why did she file suit, and why did she move her husband's body? Because the cemetery was building a mausoleum in front of his burial place, and that was going to block the view from his grave. And what was the view from his grave? The access ramp to the Major Deegan Expressway.

One Saturday night, I attended a bat mitzvah reception, and amid everything going on, I noticed the mother of the bat mitzvah was boiling. I thought the veins in her neck were going to burst. I walked over and asked what was wrong. She told me how upset she was because the caterer had run out of lamb chops. I thought to myself, "Every bat mitzvah has trillions of details involved in it, ranging from what will she wear to will she get every musical note right to who will come and who will not come to will the pictures come out, will the food be good, will Uncle So-and-So come or stay away, will Aunt So-and-So give a chintzy present like she did last time, will the rabbi give a good sermon this time, or will he talk on and on forever like he did at so-and-so's bat mitzvah last year."

A bar or bat mitzvah has so many tense moments that someone once said to me during a bar mitzvah rehearsal, "If our marriage makes it through this bar mitzvah, we can get through anything!" And it is true: a bar or bat mitzvah is a tense moment in the life of every family because there are zillions of details involved. And it's impossible for every one of them to go right. "So," I thought to myself, "if your child makes it through the bat mitzvah and doesn't trip up even once, and if most of your relatives and friends come to the simhah and don't embarrass you or spoil the party by getting drunk, and if your dress fits and matches your shoes and your lipstick and your purse, and if your husband does what he is told to do without question, and if the food is warm and tasty (or at least some of it is), then even if one of the zillion details that go into making this simhah isn't 1000 percent perfect, don't you still have a lot to be grateful for?"

No, she was angry at the missing lamb chops.

People like Leona Helmsley, Martha Stewart, and the bat mitzvah parents have what radio talk show host Dennis Prager calls *Missing Tile Syndrome.* In his book *Happiness Is a Serious Problem*, Prager wrote the following:

> One of human nature's most effective ways of sabotaging happiness is to look at a beautiful scene and fixate on whatever is flawed or missing, no matter how small.
>
> This tendency is easily demonstrated. Imagine looking up at a tiled ceiling from which one tile is missing— you will most likely concentrate on that missing tile. In fact, the more beautiful the ceiling, the more you are likely to concentrate on the missing tile and permit it to affect your enjoyment of the rest of the ceiling.
>
> Now when it comes to ceilings or anything else that can exist in a complete form, concentrating on missing details can be desirable. We don't want a physician to overlook the slightest medical detail or a builder to overlook a single tile. But what is desirable or even necessary in the

physical world can be very self-destructive when applied to the emotional world. Ceilings can be perfect, but life cannot. In life, there will always be tiles missing—and even when there aren't, we can always imagine a more perfect life and therefore imagine that something is missing.

The Missing Tile Syndrome is ubiquitous. If you are overweight, all you see are flat stomachs and perfect physical specimens. If you have pimples, all you see is flawless skin. Women who have difficulty getting pregnant walk around seeing only pregnant women and babies. Nor do you need to be overweight, have pimples, or want a child to believe that you have a missing tile. You can allow any real—or merely perceived—flaw to diminish your happiness.[110]

Do you know a Leona Helmsley? A Martha Stewart? Someone who suffers from Missing Tile Syndrome? Someone who is never fully content? There is always something bothering them, always something to worry about, something to upset them. They're always going from one issue to the next, unable to be satisfied with where they're at or what they have. Or are you yourself like Martha and Leona? Remember what Kirk Douglas said: "Maybe when you die, you come before a big, bearded man on a big throne, and you say, 'Is this heaven?' And he says, 'Heaven? You just came from there.'"[111]

DEPENDENCE

When I was a kid my parents moved a lot—but I always found them.

—Rodney Dangerfield

In 2016, I read an article in the *New York Times* entitled "Behind Our Anxiety, the Fear of Being Unneeded."[112] It was written by the Dalai Lama. In it, he makes the case that in life there is something more important even than safety and security. The most important basic need is our need to be needed. We all want to feel like we play an important role, whether in an organization or family or in the life of another.

No wonder the Dalai Lama is so highly thought of. He understands! He understands that from the day we are born until the day we die, we all share the same trait: the need to feel needed.

Dr. Dean Ornish wrote, "Our survival depends on the healing power of love, intimacy, and relationships."[113] We need people who make us feel special and irreplaceable and who tend to our needs and banish our fears and insecurities.

Who is it that we need the most? Who is it that most needs us? A good case can be made that it is parents and children who are most dependent upon each other. I read an interview with Jerry Lewis in which he was asked, "What drives you?"

He answered, "My parents were both entertainers. But they never amounted to much. Maybe that is the reason they always put me down and always told me that I was not very good. My parents are long gone, and yet I keep thinking that if I can just perform a little bit better this time, they would look down and smile from wherever they are and they will say, 'That's good, man. You've got it! Now you're doing it right!'"

The reporter then said to him, "You have the whole world applauding for you. Isn't that enough?"

And Jerry Lewis replied, "There is no comparison between having the adulation of strangers and having the admiration of your parents. No comparison." That need never ends.

You know who was lucky? The iconic basketball player Bill Russell, who got in life what Jerry Lewis never did.

Bill Russell was one of America's most successful athletes. He won two college titles, one Olympic gold medal, and eleven NBA championships with the Boston Celtics. He was the first black NBA player enshrined in the Basketball Hall of Fame. In 2011, Russell was honored by President Barack Obama with the Presidential Medal of Freedom. When asked if this was the greatest personal honor in his life, Russell replied, "A close second." What was the first? His answer was this, as reported in the *New York Times*:

"When he was about seventy-seven, my father and I were talking," Russell answered. "And he said, 'You know, you're all grown up now, and I want to tell you something. You know, I am very proud of the way you turned out as my son, and I'm proud of you as a father.' My father is my hero, O.K., and I cannot perceive of anything topping that," Russell continued.[114]

Bill Russell himself was seventy-seven at the time he received the medal and spoke those words. Even at that late stage in life, nothing to him was more important than having received the admiration and adulation of his father.

That is why the best thing we can do when it comes to our children is to love them. This simple idea was expressed beautifully by Warren Buffet. He was asked about the best advice he had ever received, and surprisingly, his answer had nothing to do with money. He said the advice came from his father, and it was, in his words, as follows:

> The power of unconditional love. I mean, there is no power on earth like unconditional love. And I think that if you offered that to your child, I mean, you're 90 percent of the way home. There may be days when you don't feel like it—it's not uncritical love; that's a different animal—but to know you can always come back, that is huge in life. That takes you a long, long way. And I would say that every parent out there that can extend that to their child at an early age, it's going to make for a better human being.[115]

Providing our children unconditional love is not only a good thing for them; it's a good thing for us as well. It might turn out to be the best investment you make in your future because there will come a time when you are going to need unconditional love from your children.

There is an age-old worry, one where we fear that we will (but we hope that we never) have to depend upon our children. But you know what? More and more people do! When people were dying in their fifties and sixties, they might not have needed the help of their children. But now that we're living longer, into our eighties and nineties, many people find themselves needing their children. For some, that need means something as little as a ride to the doctor or taking care of some bills. For others, it can mean daily involvement.

If it were up to me, I would change the term *golden years*. Instead, I would call them the *silver years*. Gold needs almost no maintenance, whereas silver needs constant care. Silver needs to be polished; it needs attention. Gold you can buy and put away. Silver is a high-maintenance item to own. You have to maintain it, or else it will soon tarnish. In the silver years, parents need ongoing maintenance.

Being a "good kid" when you're fifteen or sixteen counts. But to be a good, devoted child when you're forty-five or fifty? That really counts!

Let us remember this fact of life: there comes a time when parents need their children. For some of us, all that's necessary is another call, another card, another invitation, another visit, another link with their grandchildren. For others, it's going to take a lot more!

Only children can give parents what no one else in our society can—not caregivers, not social clubs or agencies, not friends—a feeling of being genuinely loved and wanted. This need explains to some degree the intensity of the relationship between grandparents and grandchildren. In large part, it's because we need each other. They need our Amazon Prime password and our credit card! We need their hugs and kisses! And one thing more: our grandchildren give us—and we give them—unconditional love. That's hard to find in this world!

The simple truth is that when our children are small, they are dependent on us. But at the other end of the life cycle, we are dependent on them. For they can give us something that no doctor or nurse or retirement home or stock dividend or Medicare payment can offer: they can give us love! You may have Medicare, and Medicare may pay your medical bills, but Medicare doesn't call you on your birthday or ask you how you feel or send you a tie or sit at your bedside when you are ill. You may have stocks and bonds ... but stocks and bonds don't visit you and don't call you and don't tell you that they love you. They may send you your dividend checks every month ... but they don't enclose a personal note or a drawing by a grandchild (they don't do that on Wall Street). And therefore I tell you if you're not on good terms with your children, you go and fix it! You reach out, not because they're right but because it's the right thing for you to do. Don't keep score, don't count telephone calls, don't care whose turn it is, don't calculate who called less. Instead call, write, send, pay, call, write, send, pay. It's an investment in your future.

Some years ago, when Bear Bryant was the coach of the University of Alabama football team, he was asked to do a television commercial for Southern Bell Telephone. Coach Bryant's part in the commercial was simple. He was to have only one line. At the conclusion of the text of the commercial, Bryant was supposed to say, as though barking orders to his players, "Call your mama." However, when it came time to film the commercial, something unexpected happened. Coach Bryant turned toward the camera, tears welling up in his eyes, and he said, "Call your mama. I sure wish I could call mine."[116]

Remember what Margaret Atwood wrote in *The Handmaid's Tale*: "No mother is ever, completely, a child's idea of what a mother should be, and I suppose it works the other way around as well. But despite everything, we didn't do too badly by one another, we did as well as most."[117]

TRUTH

Our press secretary gave alternative facts.
                                    —Kellyanne Conway

There's this family who lives on a farm in America. One day, the father calls his three sons—Anthony, Louis, and Nick—into the kitchen. He says to his sons, "Which one of you pushed the outhouse into the river?"

"Not I," replies Anthony.

"Nor me," Louis says.

"It wasn't me either, Father," says Nick.

So the father says, "I want to tell you a story about George Washington. One day George Washington's father gave him a hatchet. Then George Washington chopped down his father's favorite cherry tree. George Washington's father said, 'George, who chopped down my favorite cherry tree?' George Washington replied, 'Father, I cannot tell a lie ... it was I who chopped down your cherry tree.' So George Washington's father hugged and kissed his son for being honest with him."

Then Anthony says, "Father, I, like George Washington, cannot tell a lie ... I pushed the outhouse into the river."

The father takes off his belt and starts beating him. After the beating ends, Anthony says, "But Father, I was honest like George Washington."

The father replies, "But George Washington's father wasn't in the cherry tree when he chopped it down."

The story reminds us of just how far our country has come from expecting our political leaders to tell the truth. According to the *Washington Post*, while in office as president, Donald Trump misled or lied to the American people more than 30,000 times.[118] But an even stronger indicator of how far we have come in regard to leaders telling the truth was the moment when the president's senior advisor Kellyanne Conway went on *Meet the Press* and defended White House Press Secretary Sean Spicer. He had recently issued a false statement claiming that the attendance at Trump's inauguration was larger than that of Barack Obama's. When asked why Spicer "uttered a provable falsehood," Conway responded that Spicer hadn't lied but had simply given "alternative facts."[119]

The truth of the matter is for decades now we have heard "alternative facts" coming from our political leaders on both sides of the aisle. Al Gore said he discovered the internet! FDR, when running for vice president, claimed he wrote Haiti's constitution. It never happened, but he turned out to be a pretty good president anyway. David Greenberg, a professor of history and media studies at Rutgers, put it so well: "There are lies and then there are lies, and we wouldn't be honest if we didn't acknowledge that sometimes lying—and lying well—is a necessary skill for those at the top, whether it's the kind of official deception that might be necessary to protect national security or the benignly misleading rhetoric that often accompanies a heated campaign."[120]

Understandably, it's not just politicians who lie. The first person to lie was the first person in this world! Adam, when confronted by God regarding having eaten from the Tree of Knowledge, immediately takes it like a man ... he lies and blames it on his wife! Alternative facts have been with us since time immemorial.

Lots of people claim to have never told a lie, but studies show that we all tell lies several times a day, often to those closest to us—our partners, friends, and children. "White lies," which are thought to be of little consequence, are an example. If we were brutally honest all the time, few of us could survive. I read a death notice of a man who died because he told the truth. His wife had asked him if he would still love her when she was old, fat, and ugly. He meant to say, "Of course I will," but it came out as "Of course I do!" Services were held for him last Thursday at Beth David Cemetery in Long Island.

So yes, sometimes a lie is an absolute necessity. Just ask God.

God tells Sarah that she is to have a child. Sarah laughs, saying, "My husband is too old to make this happen." God, in repeating this story to Abraham, tells him that Sarah said she was too old to bear a child. God used an alternate fact! He didn't tell the true story so as to spare Abraham embarrassment and to avoid any conflict with his wife.

With all this in mind, perhaps it would be best to adhere to the following rules when it comes to alternative facts:

Don't lie to yourself. To thine own self be true.

Never lie just to make yourself look good, because you will end up looking like a fool.

While you can't lie to make yourself look good, you can—at times—lie to make others feel good. If your friend bought a "no return" dress, tell her it looks good ... even if it doesn't!

There are times when we may have to use alternative facts, but don't do it too often, because it can become a bad habit.

Be aware that a lie can take on a life of its own, that it can grow and infect a whole society, that it can replace a necessary truth. In 2020, many years after Donald Trump's claim that Barack Obama was born in Kenya had been proven false, a majority of Republicans still believed it to be true.

Walter Scott told the truth when he wrote, "Oh what a tangled web we weave, when first we practice to deceive."[121]

Remember what Chuck Todd, host of *Meet the Press*, said in response to Kellyanne Conway: "Alternative facts? Alternative facts are not facts. They are falsehoods."

LETTING GO

The Five Most Important Stages in the Life of an Actor, according to Hugh O'Brian:

Who is Hugh O'Brian?
Get me Hugh O'Brian as the star of our next picture!
Get me somebody who's a Hugh O'Brian type.
Get me a young Hugh O'Brian.
Who WAS Hugh O'Brian?

In the Jewish tradition, when you go to a cemetery to bury a loved one, as you carry the casket to its final resting place, it is the custom to pause and make seven stops along the way. There's a beautiful and relevant explanation for this. The seven stops are meant to represent the seven stages in life that we pass through from birth to death. And for each one of these stages, we have to learn to stop and let go before we can move on to the next stage. From childhood to adolescence to early adulthood to middle age to old age to all points in between, there are moments in life when we must face the fact that time moves on ... and so must we. And in order for us to do this in a well-adjusted manner, we've got to let go of that previous stage in life that is no more.

This "letting go" is not easy.

147

It's not easy when you have to let go of the keys of your car and give them to your sixteen-year-old kid. But it's even more painful when you're eighty-six, and your kid asks you to give him the keys to your car for good. It's not easy to let go of those keys when you feel like you're basically giving away your independence. It's like the elderly man telling his friend, "I've had two bypass surgeries, a hip replacement, new knees, prostate cancer, and diabetes. I'm half-blind, can't hear anything quieter than a jet engine, take forty different medications that make me dizzy, have bouts with dementia, poor circulation, can hardly feel my hands and feet anymore, can't remember if I'm eighty-five or ninety-two, have lost all my friends ... but thank God I still have my driver's license!"

It's not easy admitting you ain't what you used to be. Letting go of power, coming to terms with old age, and making peace with reality is enormously difficult. "I built this business ... I raised this family ... I created this institution, and now I'm going to let it go? I'm going to turn it over to someone else?" That's not easy to do. But we've got to learn to do it!

It's very hard letting go of our children at every stage in life. It's hard to let go of their hands when they cross the street by themselves for the first time. It's hard to let go of their hands as they walk into school for the first time. It's hard to let go when you give them the keys to the car and they're truly on their own for the first time. And it's hard to let go of our children's hands as they walk down the aisle into the waiting arms of their new husband or wife.

Erich Fromm, in his book *Sane Society*, underscored the deeply tragic character of Mother Love, which in our day I believe pertains to Father Love as well.[122] The dilemma is this: Love normally seeks to hold tight, to grow together! In the love between husband and wife, for instance, they look forward to an ever-growing closeness in the course of years. With a child, however, a new element enters. The parent loves the child selflessly and passionately. Yet this love is doomed from the outset because the parent cannot expect to grow constantly closer to the child as time goes on (and that is the tragedy Fromm described). A parent's love, which holds tight, must learn to let go. The parent must help the child grow away in order to allow them to grow up.

Of course, in some ways, we never let go. An op-ed article in the *New York Times* entitled "A Parent Is Always a Parent" told of a successful psychiatrist who, in his fifties, took his mother, who was almost an octogenarian, to a performance given by the Metropolitan Opera in New York's Lincoln Center. After the last curtain came down and they were making their way out the lobby to his Mercedes, she turned to him and said, "Did you go to the bathroom?" Some things never change!

But when it comes to our children, many things have to, as the poet Kahlil Gibran wrote so beautifully:

Your children are not your children.
They are the sons and daughters of life's longing for itself.
You may give them your love but not your thoughts,
For they have their own thoughts.
You may strive to be like them,
but seek not to make them like you,
For life goes not backward nor tarries with yesterday.[123]

There are three things we owe our children: dedication, education, and abdication. Abdication, it would seem, is the most difficult of all.

Hugh O'Brian was most famous for playing Wyatt Earp on television. When the real Wyatt Earp grew old and had to hang up his spurs, he moved from Tombstone to Los Angeles, where he earned a living as an unpaid consultant for silent cowboy movies. Time marches on, and so must we. We would be smart to keep in mind the words of Judith Viorst, from her outstanding book *Necessary Losses*: "At each stage of our life, we are going to be confronted with experiences that will require us to say good-bye; that will require us to relinquish something we may not want to relinquish; that will require us to move on whether we are ready for it or not. And yet if we can do that without denying it, fighting it, refusing it, we grow."[124]

Remember what Keith Urban (or possibly Rumi) wrote: "Life is a balance of holding on and letting go."

WORDS TO LIVE BY

FUHGEDABOUDIT

Once a woman has forgiven her man, she must not reheat
his sins for breakfast.

—Marlene Dietrich

D o you remember the Barry Levinson movie *Avalon*? In one
scene, the family is having Thanksgiving dinner, and one of
the uncles comes late, and he is the one who traditionally cuts the
turkey. They get tired of waiting for him, so someone else finally
cuts the turkey. And as soon as he does, the uncle arrives and says,
"You cut the turkey without me?" And from then on, there is only
acrimony. Never again does the family sit down to eat at the same
table—never again until death brings them together. But by then
it is too late. At the shiva table, they cry for all the meals they
could have had together before this one, and all the years they
wasted just because somebody cut the turkey too soon.

I know lots of families that have uncles like that; once you cut the
turkey before he gets there, or once you sit him at the wrong table at a
wedding or bat mitzvah, he is never able to see that no one meant him
any harm, that no one wanted to wrong him, that it was just one of
those things. But he just can't let go of it. To him, everyone is out to
get him, when in reality, he is the only one hurting himself.

That's the problem with anger, resentment, an unwillingness to forgive. After all is said and done, we end up hurting ourselves the most. I know many people who say of someone who hurt them, "They don't deserve to be forgiven." *They* may not deserve it, but *you* do! Forgiveness is for the forgiver, not the forgiven. The person who has hurt you does not deserve the right to continue to hurt you. Life is too short to waste by giving it away to someone who hurt you.

In the bestseller *Tuesdays with Morrie*, Mitch Albom wrote about forgiveness:

> I watched my old college professor, Morrie Schwartz, who was dying from ALS, break into tears when he told me of an old friend with whom he had lost touch. Once they had been so close. But a silly little argument had split them apart. "I found out last year," Morrie said, "that this friend died of cancer." He began to weep openly. "I never had the chance to make it up to him. I never had the chance to say, 'I'm sorry.' Why did I let that stupid argument separate us for all these years?" I watched Morrie cry. He could no longer move his arms or legs, he was weeks away from death, but he wept not for his weakened health, but for the missed opportunity. He wept for the days, weeks, and years that he could have spent in loving companionship with a friend, but instead lost to stubbornness. "If there's anyone you care about that you're fighting with now," Morrie told me, "let it go. Say you were wrong—even if you think you're right. Because I promise you, when you get to this point in your life"—he nodded to his dying body—"you won't care who was right or wrong. You'll only want to savor every minute you had with them."[125]

Living in New York is not easy. It's a constant challenge. You're packed together on the trains like sardines, with people bumping into you. You find yourself, at times, stepping over people sleeping on the street. You have to encounter panhandlers and constantly be on the lookout because people don't always curb their dogs. Taxi drivers are argumentative. Other drivers think their cars are Sherman tanks. So watch out! If you live in New York, it feels as if there are daily assaults on your personal dignity and divine image. And yet before the pandemic, New York was blossoming: the crime rate was down, its economy up! And some of that was the result, in part, of New Yorkers having developed the ability to confront all the assaults on their dignity by echoing one word. The word is spelled f-u-h-g-e-d-a-b-o-u-d-i-t, and it's pronounced "forget about it!"

Maybe that's what motivated Roberto Alomar and John Hirschbeck to reconcile. Roberto Alomar, second baseman for the Baltimore Orioles, attained a measure of infamy in 1996 when, in an argument with umpire John Hirschbeck, he spit in Hirschbeck's face. That scene was replayed time and again before millions of viewers. But you know what? Some years later they made up ... they realized that forgiveness is good for the liver—in both senses of the word! Hirschbeck said, "If that's the worst thing Robbie ever does in his life, he'll lead a real good life. People make mistakes. You forgive, you forget, and you move on."[126]

Did the person with whom you are angry do anything as bad as spit in your face? Forgive them ... for your sake—not theirs. It's good for the liver ... in both senses of the phrase.

It's even good for those no longer among the living. Psychiatrists' offices are filled with people still carrying grievances with parents who are gone. None of us are saints ... and none of our parents were saints! We all have our moments in which we take pride, and we all have moments that brought out the worst in us. Our parents and loved ones grew up in times very different from ours, and those times affected their personalities and character. Some were stingy and others unemotional, some quick tempered and others abusive. And some of us carry those wounds throughout our lives. When you really think about it, that serves no purpose.

No matter what someone else has done to you, the only person hurt by your anger and resentment is you. Fuhgedaboudit! In the act of forgiving another, we free ourselves from the debilitating effects of chronic anger and resentment. I know it is easier said than done. We've been hurt, abused, offended, and bruised. Forget about it? How can we? The answer is this: you have to work at it!

The celebrated philosopher Immanuel Kant was once jolted by the discovery that his servant, Lampe, whom he had trusted implicitly for many years, had in fact been robbing him steadily and systematically. Kant had no choice but to dismiss him despite his heavy dependence on him. Understandably, Kant did miss him terribly. In the philosopher's journal, we read the echo of his sadness when he wrote to himself, "Remember to forget Lampe."[127]

Yes, sometimes in order to maintain our equilibrium and happiness, it becomes vital for us to make sure that we remember to forget. A scientific paper in *Neuron* argued that forgetting outdated memories lets the brain clear out details that don't matter so people can adapt to newer information and make more intelligent decisions.

Indeed, the Kabbalists powerfully make this point when they tell us in the Zohar that the Hebrew word for joy and happiness, *simcha*, comes from the word *sh'mocho*—"he blots out." We will never be able to enjoy the happy moments of life unless we are first able to blot out from memory those moments in life that caused us pain and anguish.

Remember what Carrie Fisher quoted in her novel *The Best Awful*: "Resentment is like drinking poison and waiting for the other person to die."[128]

THAT'S LIFE

It is what it is.

—Al Gore, Donald Rumsfeld, Alex
Rodriguez, Angelina Jolie, et al.

The expression *It is what it is* has almost become the core mantra of the twenty-first century. No one is sure where the phrase comes from. In a 2006 column, *New York Times* word maven William Safire wrote that the first use he uncovered was in the *Nebraska State Journal* in 1949, in a piece about pioneer life.[129] But he suspected that its origins went further back. Maybe to the seventeenth century? In *An Essay Concerning Human Understanding*, philosopher John Locke wrote that "Essence may be taken for the very being of anything, whereby it is what it is."

It's doubtful whether modern adherents to this mantra know they are quoting Locke, but the message is clear nonetheless. Al Gore said it when he learned he had lost the 2000 presidential election. Angelina Jolie said it when asked if she minded being branded the "other woman" in the Brad Pitt–Jennifer Aniston split. Donald Rumsfeld said it before the United States attacked Baghdad. Alex Rodriguez said it after making a costly error in a playoff game.

"It is what it is." The words are simple, but they constitute an important stepping-stone to happiness. They capture an all-important mindset that tells us there are certain things in life beyond our control. Faye Dunaway said it all: "You can't take responsibility for everything. You can't have that kind of control. At some point it's all out of our hands." If you ever hope to achieve some measure of happiness in life, you're just going to have to accept that.

COVID-19 reminded us all that things are often out of our hands. It also emphasized that "it is what it is" also means that life isn't fair sometimes. During the pandemic, for example, some countries were badly infected while the country next door wasn't. Why? Listen to these words from the *New York Times*: "Most experts agree that there may be no single reason for some countries to be hit and others missed. The answer likely to be some combination of above factors, as well as one other mentioned by researchers: sheer luck."[130]

Since luck is always a factor, when things go wrong, there is one question not to ask and one answer not to give.

The question not to ask is "Why me?" Why you? Why anyone? Why is a one-year-old baby hooked up to monitors and IV drips in a pediatric oncology center? There are many things in life over which we have absolutely no control. When you are sick and go to the doctor, he doesn't ask you if you've been good or bad; the doctor asks you for a family history because our genetic makeup dictates, in large part, whether we will be healthy or sick, whether a growth is malignant or benign. There are more than eight billion people living on Planet Earth, and 99.9 percent of your genes are the same as everyone else's. The difference is in the remaining 0.1 percent. And there is nothing we can do about it.

The answer not to give when things go wrong is this: "Everything happens for a reason."

Just ask Kate Bowler. Kate Bowler is a professor in the History of Christianity Department at Duke University. In 2015, when she was only thirty-five, she was suddenly and unexpectedly diagnosed with stage IV cancer. She wrote a bestselling book about her experience, and in it she includes a list of ten things people shouldn't say to a person experiencing such a crisis, one of which is this unhelpful (and inaccurate) panacea: "Everything happens for a reason." In fact, she titled her book *Everything Happens for a Reason: And Other Lies I've Loved*.[131]

You want proof that she's right, that there's often no reason why things happen? Try this one: three days after the US bombing of Hiroshima, our planes took off on a mission to drop another atom bomb on a different Japanese city. You know what the name of that city was? Kuroko! That's right, not Nagasaki … Kuroko! What happened was because there were heavy clouds over Kuroko, a split-second decision was made to bomb Nagasaki instead. So some fifty thousand people lost their lives in Nagasaki, while some fifty thousand people in Kuroko were saved … for a reason? Everything happens for a reason? You will never convince me of that!

No matter how good you may be, it can't guarantee that, in the blink of an eye, in minutes, something won't occur to change your whole world and you will find yourself wondering how it happened so fast. Some say this is a black swan event—a rare, unexpected, and potentially devastating occurrence. I say that's life!

That's the reality of life. For better and for worse, we don't always get what we deserve in this world. Good people can get incurable illnesses, and bad people can remain healthy. Yes, bad things happen to good people! That's life! I always think back to the words of Malcolm Forbes Jr., who spent millions of his billion-dollar fortune running for president. He was once asked what he thought was the key to becoming rich, and he answered, "To be born to a wealthy father." He's right! But that's not fair. His father left him bundles of bucks, and my father left me cases of books. His father left him potential for billions; my father left me potential for diabetes! There is so much in our lives over which we have no control.

Yes, you can believe in God. You can be good and righteous and in tip-top shape, but when you really think about it, we are all just one call away, one doctor's visit away, one moment away from our lives changing in ways we never could have imagined. All of us at some point in life must go from happiness to sorrow, from health to sickness, from life to death in a split second. Or, to put it in not-so-delicate terms, one day you can be flying high like a pigeon … and the next day you can be the statue.

Do right because it's the right thing to do. Take to heart the words from chapter one of *Ethics of the Fathers.* Shimon the Righteous would say, "Do not be as slaves, who serve their master for the sake of reward. Rather, be as slaves who serve their master not for the sake of reward. And the fear of Heaven should be upon you."[132]

This is the human condition.

Remember what Johnny Carson said: "If life was fair, Elvis would be alive and all the impersonators would be dead."

RERUNS

It ain't over till it's over.

—Yogi Berra

"It is what it is" is not the whole story! Because there is another often-quoted popular phrase that tells us of another "it" that is likewise a necessary ingredient for happiness. What is this "it"? "It ain't over till it's over!"

It was the great "philosopher" Yogi Berra who gave these words to the world, but they are very much in keeping with ancient religious traditions, which tell us that while it may be difficult, if not impossible, to change our circumstances and to changes our loved ones, we can, in fact, change ourselves. And it's never too late to do so!

Just ask Bill Wilson—the man known to legions of alcoholics as Bill W. There is a book about him written by Susan Cheever, whose father—the noted writer John Cheever—was an alcoholic who taught his daughter how to mix a martini by the age of six. In 1934, Bill W.'s doctors concluded that he was a hopeless drunk and told his wife that there was no cure for him, except for putting him into an asylum. Wilson had checked himself into hospitals three times, all to no avail. As Cheever wrote, "The more he decided not to drink, the more irresistible drinks seemed to become."[133] Then a friend told him of the work of the eminent psychiatrist Carl Jung and the American psychiatrist William James, who had both come to the conclusion that only God could give one strength to stop drinking. Wilson never had another drink. One thing led to another ... and Alcoholics Anonymous was started, and countless people's lives have been changed for the better because of it. All because of Bill Wilson!

I found his story interesting, but that's not what fascinated me. What fascinated me was the description of Bill Wilson on his deathbed. A lifelong smoker, he had been fighting emphysema for years, and now he was losing the battle. On his deathbed, Christmas Day of 1970, he wrote a note to his nurse asking for three shots of whiskey. And he was upset when he didn't get them. A week later, he asked for booze again, and then a week later, and then a week later. He had been sober for thirty-four years, and yet he wanted a drink. In fact, he had wanted a drink every day of his life.

Yes, it's not easy to change. Every day it's a battle! Bill Wilson had a propensity to drink. He couldn't get rid of it, but he was able to control it. All of us have certain propensities and inclinations and desires, whether they're the result of our nature or our nurture, and it is not easy to change. Whether you're a drinker or stingy or selfish or an abusive spouse, an absent parent, or disrespectful to your parents—changing will be a battle every day of your life.

But the battle can be won; we can change ... if we want to. HBO once had a special featuring Kirk Douglas and his son, Michael. Theirs was not always a good relationship. Kirk Douglas was not always a good father, and Michael not always a good son. When Kirk Douglas suffered a stroke in 1996, he became a different man.

Toward the end of the program, Kirk asked Michael, "Was I a good father?"

And Michael answered, "You have ultimately been a great father."

Not all of us have been good at all the roles we have to play, but it ain't over till it's over. Ultimately we can be remembered as having been great at what we did. We have to work on our "ultimately." We don't have to let what we have been define what we will be. When we allow ourselves to believe that it ain't over till it's over, then we get to keep waking up and trying again.

Let's learn from Maxcy Filer. His one desire in life was to become a lawyer. He took the bar examination in California and failed. So he took it again. And he failed. For twenty-four years, Maxcy Filer took the bar examination in California every six months … and failed it every time. But on his forty-ninth attempt, he passed it.[134] At the age of sixty-one, when he was sworn in as a lawyer, he got a standing ovation from his colleagues, and rightfully so. I may not want to use him as my lawyer, but he deserves that standing ovation! He is the embodiment of *try, try again*.

None of us are robots or puppets. We are human beings, and as such, we are not only shaped by our environment, but we also shape it. We are not only the creatures of circumstances; we create circumstances. We are not only responsible for our past; we are also capable of changing our future. We can change if we realize it ain't over till it's over!

I know of a man who made his living as a smuggler and a crook, a man who cheated on his wife with every floozy he could find, a man who wheeled and dealed and bribed his way through life, a man who indulged in good food, fine wine, and fine women. And one day he changed. He set himself to saving the lives of 1,100 Jews. His name? Oskar Schindler.

It ain't over till it's over!

Remember what Nora Ephron said in her 1996 commencement address at Wellesley College: "You can always change your mind. I know: I've had four careers and three husbands."[135]

FLIP-FLOP

What you see from here you don't see from there.
   —Ariel Sharon, on becoming prime minister of Israel

I t's not a compliment to call someone a *flip-flopper*. To many, it is a sign of wishy-washiness, a sign of someone without principles. But the truth is flip-flopping is an important illustration of growth.

Ariel Sharon was once known as the "father of the settlement movement" in Israel. When he served as minister of housing for the Israeli government in the 1990s, more Israeli houses were built in the West Bank and Gaza than at any other time since the Six-Day War. In 1998, when he served as Israel's foreign minister, he said, "Everyone there should move, should run, should grab more hills, expand the territory. Everything that's grabbed will be in our hands. Everything we don't grab will be in their hands."[136]

This very same man, the one who had once said to grab everything, flip-flopped after becoming prime minister and unilaterally gave back the entire Gaza Strip and dismantled the Israeli settlements there.

Talk about a flip-flop! How do you explain it? Let me tell you how he explains it. It's found in these succinct words of his: "What you see from here [the prime minister's chair] you don't see from there."[137] That is, when you're the prime minister, you have a different view, one you were unable to see until that moment. You are privy to different information. You have a different perspective. And because of that, sometimes you have to flip-flop on some strongly held past beliefs. Even if you're now a very public figure whose changing perspective is likely to generate stiff criticism.

And what about us? The Talmud tells us, "As people age their opinions change."

One of the worst things a person can say is "That's just the way I am ... take it or leave it." It's true that to some extent, all of us will always be the way we are because our basic natures do not change, but it is equally true for all of us that we must grow, and with growth comes (hopefully) a little more perspective, a little more wisdom.

Change is always possible; flip-flops are necessary if we are to grow and, what's more, if we are to acknowledge that we have grown. Barry Goldwater, one time a famously right-wing conservative, later in life was a major advocate for gays being accepted in the army. Supreme Court Justice Harry Blackmun was the one who wrote the brief in favor of capital punishment, but years later, he said he would never do that again.

Bestselling author Philip Roth once revealed something very intimate about himself in an interview with *Entertainment Weekly*. He described how eight years earlier, he had dumped his longtime team, the New York Mets, and become a Yankees fan. In his words, "It's one of the smartest things I've ever done ... I thought I didn't have to be loyal to my playground allegiances anymore. I was moving on!"[138] I personally think switching his loyalty from the Mets to the Yankees was one of the dumbest things he's ever done! But I can't argue with the idea that one does not have to always remain loyal to their "playground allegiances." One should most certainly know how to move on.

There is a legend that says when Alexander the Great was first serving in the Greek army, one of his superiors insulted him, and Alexander promised revenge someday. Later on in life, when he became the ruler of the Greek empire, one of his aides remarked to him how he had never taken vengeance on his one-time adversary. And Alexander replied, "I am not going to allow Alexander the Small to dictate policy to Alexander the Great." Yes, for Alexander the Great—like for Ariel Sharon—the view had changed between "here" and "there."

Are you still looking at things the same way? When was the last time you changed the brand of mayonnaise you use? Or changed to a different news program? The more we allow ourselves to be flexible, the more likely our view is to change—a powerful impetus for growth and, hopefully, happiness.

Remember what Stephen Colbert said about George W. Bush: "He believes the same thing Wednesday that he believed on Monday—no matter what happened on Tuesday."[139]

COMPLAINING

People won't have time for you if you are always angry or complaining.

—Stephen Hawking

Stephen Hawking was a genius who changed the way we view the world, and you don't need to be an astrophysicist to appreciate how sharp his mind was. That insightfulness is just as clear in his comment about complaining: "People won't have time for you if you are always angry or complaining." I wish some of my own people were as wise.

It's one of the most popular Hebrew songs, and it's one of the best-known Hebrew words. It's a word that takes five English words to translate. The word is *dayenu*, and the translation is "It would have been enough." *Dayenu* comes from the Passover Haggadah, but it is well known by Jew and non-Jew alike. You hear it sung at Jewish weddings and celebrations because every Jew knows the tune, and every Jew knows the words. What they don't know is that the poem providing its context and meaning is just not true!

Dayenu is a song of praise and gratitude to the Almighty. We thank God for giving us the manna and splitting the sea and drowning our enemies and taking care of us in the desert and giving us the Sabbath and the Torah and the land of Israel. Each step of the way, we say, "Dayenu." Had you just done this, Lord, it would have been enough to merit our gratitude.

That's what we say, but that's not what our ancestors did! On the contrary, they had one complaint after the other. Three days after crossing the Red Sea, they were already complaining about the water. And then they complained about the food. And then they complained about the accommodations. One complaint after the other! No gratitude, no appreciation, no dayenu!

And this is not simply my modern-day viewpoint of the text! This is the viewpoint of King David. Read Psalm 106, where he tells us, "Our fathers understood not thy wonders in Egypt; they remembered not the multitude of thy mercies; but provoked him at the sea, even at the Red Sea."

Yes, our people were complaining then, and they seem to have continued the tradition to this very day. There is a book about the Yiddish language entitled *Born to Kvetch*, written by Michael Wex.[140] It's a wonderful book, extremely well done. In fact, I liked everything about the book except for the title: *Born to Kvetch*. Why, of all Yiddish words, was this the one the author chose as being most representative of the Yiddish language? After all, he could just as well have called the book *Born to Be a Mensch*. But obviously he felt—and I think many others do as well—that kvetching and complaining are almost a genetic condition among Jews.

As a rabbi, I see it all the time! People come to me frequently with ongoing complaints. To tell you the truth, the complaints would concern me, the complaints would bother me, except for the fact that they all seem to be coming from the same people! Besides, Dale Carnegie got it right when he wrote in his famous book *How to Win Friends and Influence People*, "Any fool can criticize, condemn, and complain—and most fools do."[141] These people can be described with a most picturesque Yiddish phrase: *ah farkrimte ponim.* It translates loosely as *the person with the perpetual scowl, the long face, the sourpuss, the person who carries an eternal chip on his shoulder.* It's the person who, when you say something positive, responds with a dim view, the grim, the negative, the sarcastic. It's the kind of person who is much like both halves of the couple who, after completing a meal in a restaurant, were asked by the waiter, "Was *anything* okay?"

Is complaining part of our people's DNA? I might have thought so until I read an article in a Mormon journal *Public Square Magazine* entitled "Thou Shalt Not Whine," where the author, Dan Ellsworth, begins by saying, "To complain is a normal human response to the difficulties of life. But Christians have in scripture a contrast between the spiritually healthy practice of lament, and the soul-corroding practice of murmuring."[142] There you have it! Mormons also complain!

And it's not just the Mormons!

Let me tell you about Reverend William Bowen, the minister of Christ Church Unity in Kansas City, Missouri. Reverend Bowen has a congregation that sometimes complains. His people sometimes complain that the services are too long, that the music is too dull, that the sermon is boring, and even that the refreshments are not always very good. Nothing like that could ever happen here in my congregation, but this is what was happening in Reverend Bowen's church.

And so he decided to take some action to stop this complaining.[143] He gave his people bracelets to wear, bracelets embossed with the words *A complaint-free world!* And he told them to wear them and see if they could refrain from complaining for twenty-one days (because it is estimated that it takes twenty-one days to break a habit). If they failed, if they complained even once during the twenty-one days, they had to switch the bracelet to their other hand and start all over again.

And the idea somehow caught on. People heard about it and began writing in and asking for the bracelets. He was on the *Today* show, in *People* magazine, and on *Oprah* talking about this idea, and as a result, more than a million people from all over the world wrote in asking if they could have a bracelet.

I was one of them. I happily made a donation, and I wore the bracelet for twenty-one days and didn't have to move it at all. I knew I wouldn't, because you're reading the words of someone who doesn't have a complaint in the world! Do you know why? Because I remember the words of football coach Lou Holtz: "Don't burden people with your complaints. Ninety percent of the people you meet don't care about your troubles. The other ten percent are glad you have them."[144]

Dayenu … enough complaining. Whether you have a bracelet or not, now is as good a time as any to do your share to make this a "complaint-free world."

Remember what Laura Ingraham said: "There's a rule of thumb in politics. If you're at a point where you're complaining about the other guy being mean and unfair and uncivil, that's probably a sign that you're losing."[145]

FOCUS

Keep your eyes on the prize.
              —Mahalia Jackson, Duke Ellington,
                        Bruce Springsteen, et al.

Adapted from the hymn "Keep Your Hand on the Plough" by civil rights activist Alice Wine, the words *keep your eyes on the prize* have been used as a battle cry by hundreds of people, some famous, and some less so. It is a call to never give up, despite the obstacles we confront in life. It encourages us to keep focused on the goals we've set and not to be discouraged by the stumbling blocks we might encounter.

In our day and age, the words *keep your eyes on the prize* have taken on new meaning because we live in an era of what has been called *fatal distraction*.

"Fatal Distraction" is the title of a Pulitzer Prize–winning article Gene Weingarten wrote for the *Washington Post* in 2010.[146] It tells the story of a forty-nine-year-old man, Miles Harrison, described as an "amiable person, a diligent businessman, and a doting, conscientious father," who sat in a courtroom crying, charged with manslaughter. What was his crime? One day he was driving his son, Chase, to day care, and he got caught up in phone call

175

after phone call on his cell phone, and he simply forgot to drop off his two-year-old son! He went into work, forgetting his son. The child was strapped into that car seat for nearly nine hours in his office parking lot and slowly sweltered to death. A nurse testifying at the trial started to cry, describing what the father was like in the emergency room: "He would not speak at all for the longest time, not until the nurse sank down beside him and held his hand. It was only then that the patient began to open up, and what he said was that he didn't want any sedation, that he didn't deserve a respite from pain, that he wanted to feel it all, and then to die."

Who forgets a child in the back of a car? We might not want to imagine we could do such a thing, but Mr. Weingarten observed in his article:

> The wealthy do, it turns out. And the poor, and the middle class. Parents of all ages and ethnicities do it. Mothers are just as likely to do it as fathers. It happens to the chronically absent-minded and to the fanatically organized, to the college-educated and to the marginally literate. In the last 10 years, it has happened to a dentist. A postal clerk. A social worker. A police officer. An accountant. A soldier. A paralegal. An electrician. A Protestant clergyman. A rabbinical student. A nurse. A construction worker. An assistant principal. It happened to a mental health counselor, a college professor and a pizza chef. It happened to a pediatrician. It happened to a rocket scientist.

We have to face that this could happen to any of us living in the kind of world we live in.

As Avi Shuman wrote in an op-ed in Israel Hayom (as quoted in a *Times of Israel* article), "When the cell phone turns into a central tool in our lives, it's purportedly possible to understand that our head is no longer here. We receive calls every moment, text messages and emails, we take our work home with us. We're never 100% focused on the thing happening here and now."[147]

Do those words not describe how many of us are currently living our lives? In these days of fatal distraction, we have forgotten to keep our eyes on the prize. While we're looking at our tablets and iPads, screens and monitors, our kids are growing up right before our very eyes. But that's the problem—they are sitting in the back seat, and we're forgetting that they are there!

When I was a child, our major family activity was going for a ride! It was a family activity—my father got behind the wheel to drive, my mother sat next to him to tell him how to drive, and my brothers and I were scrunched together in the back seat. And when we would begin to get restless and act up—usually about two minutes into the ride—my father would say, "Don't make me come back there!" Or my mother would say, "Do you want us to turn around and go back home?" Or both of them would say, "If my hand could reach back there … "

Today families travel differently. The minivan is an apartment on wheels—spacious, with stereo sound and video monitors. There is room for everyone to do their own thing, and no longer do parents have to make conversation with their children or play word games or test them on how many state capitals they know. Now, all they have to do is pop in a video, and off they go! And this is considered progress.

In Israel, to make sure parents don't forget their children in the back seat, an app was developed called the Baby Minder; it uses GPS mapping, alerts, and other tricks to ensure that drivers keep their babies-on-board at the forefront of their minds. So how are you to be a successful parent in this multitasking day and age? Get the right app! But how many apps can you have and still remain focused? How much attention are you paying to your family during dinner if you are checking your emails under the table?

Did you ever wonder why the lion tamer in the circus goes into the cage with certain things? Really, didn't you wonder? A whip or a gun we can understand, but why a chair? And the chair always has the legs facing the lion. Did you ever wonder why? It's because the lion tries to look at all four points of the legs at once and thus forgets to focus on eating the lion tamer. The distractions deprive the lion of a kill even while they protect the lion tamer.

With all our apps and lists and appointments and Netflix, we are losing sight of what really counts. We are fatally distracted when what we should really be doing is keeping our eyes on the prize.

Remember what Bruce Lee said: "The successful warrior is the average man with laser-like focus."[148]

BUCKET LIST

BUCKET LIST
Bucket of fried chicken
Bucket of shrimp
Bucket of tartar sauce
Bucket of chili
Bucket of popcorn
Bucket of cholesterol medicine

—Homer Simpson

Sam was almost eighty-five years old and living in Florida. The years, as they inevitably do, were catching up with him, and he wasn't getting out as often as he used to. The friends he liked to kibitz with over lunch decided that with Sam's eighty-fifth birthday coming up, they would chip in and give him a special treat. They hired a beautiful woman to go to Sam's apartment to provide him with one last fling. Sure enough, she came to the apartment and rang the bell, and Sam, aided by his walker, opened the door.

He asked, "Who are you?"

She said, "I've been sent by your friends to give you super sex."

Sam looked at her and sheepishly responded, "I think I'll take the soup."

And thus began the sermon I gave on the occasion of my seventieth birthday.

Time is definitely marching on. For all of us. Steve Jobs once said, "My favorite things in life don't cost any money … it's really clear that the most precious resource we all have is time." Time is more than seconds, hours, days, and years. Time is life … time is past, present, future. And it keeps on moving. The present is already past. Time never ends, but we do. We simply run out of time! With this in mind, at the age of seventy, I decided it was time for me to create my own "bucket list."

You know what a bucket list is? It is a list of things you want to do before you "kick the bucket"! I gave that some thought, and I really couldn't come up with much. I had done most everything I could have hoped for and more. So I checked with Google to see what it had about "bucket lists." The first bucket list that came up was this: "101 Things to Do Before You Die."[149] I looked at my watch, and I realized that I didn't have time to do 101 things, so I focused on the first five suggestions:

Travel all around the world. Well, I have done my fair share of traveling, and there are still a few places that I intend to visit. But there are a lot of places I have no interest in seeing. I have no desire to travel around the world! I especially have no desire to go to New Jersey!

Learn a new language. I'm still having trouble learning Hebrew! And some of my congregation have pointed out to me that my English is not the greatest … so we'll skip that one!

Try a profession in a different field. There are some people who, I am sure, wish I would do this one! But being a rabbi continues to be a thrilling and fulfilling experience for me, and I really don't know how to do much else, so I intend to keep on going.

Achieve your ideal weight. I thought that happened only when you actually die.

Run a marathon. That is when you die!

Clearly, this kind of bucket list is not for me! The fact is I already know the things I am going to be doing in the years ahead. I am going to spend my time doing what I've always been doing. I guess I'm like the character Steve McQueen described in the movie *The Magnificent Seven*: "Reminds me of the fellow back home that fell off of a ten-story building. As he was falling, people on each floor kept hearing him say, 'So far, so good!'" Yes, for me, so far, so good! And I intend to keep it that way as long as I can.

So I made my own list, a different kind of bucket list. This is a list of things I'm *not* going to do. With the clock ticking, I decided I needed a list of things that are a waste of time and that should be avoided at all costs.

I'm not going to tell my children what to do. I had plenty of time to do that. They know where I stand. At some point, you have to accept that just like many of us have chosen to live differently from the way our parents lived, so our children are going to live differently from the way we do. As someone once put it, "Toys'R'Us—children are not."

I'm not going to wait for a thank-you from them—or from anyone! Whatever we do, we should do because we want to do it or because we have to do it. And we must not wait for a letter of gratitude for having done it. You know how slow the mail is these days.

I'm not going to live in the past. It is a waste of the present and of the future. "I should have … I could have … I would have … " brings no happiness or satisfaction to anyone.

I'm not going to try to change my spouse. A person's behavior can be modified but not their nature. We need to accept people as they are and learn to value them in all their contradictory complexity. Besides, if I try to change my wife … she'll try to change me!

I'm not going to be envious. What do I have to be envious of? I have more than my parents had and more than I ever dreamed of having. There is always going to be someone who has more. So what?

A young Nelson Rockefeller was sailing his toy boat on a pond when another boy asked, "Where's your yacht?"

"Whaddaya think I am?" Rockefeller replied. "A Vanderbilt?"

I'm not going to carry grudges. They serve no purpose. The person who hurt me should have no power over my thoughts. Take the case of former White House press secretary James Brady, whose life was never the same after he was shot by John Hinckley. When Brady was asked if he was bitter toward Mr. Hinckley, he replied, "Well, it's not classy to be bitter, and I try to be classy."[150] We all ought to try to be classy.

I'm not going to waste time thinking about death. French philosopher Montaigne said it was impossible not to think about death, so he suggested this approach: "Let us frequent it, let us get used to it, let us have nothing more often in mind than death."[151] I don't know about you, but I would have hated to be Madame Montaigne! Who wants to live with someone who is always thinking about death?

I think Jack Nicholson got it just right when he said, "We live, we die and the wheels on the bus go round and round."[152] That's life!

So if I'm not going to waste my time
telling my kids what to do,
waiting for expressions of gratitude,
trying to change my spouse,
getting stuck in the past,
being envious,
carrying a grudge,
or thinking about death,

then what am I going to do with all the time on my hands?

Well, ever since I became a grandfather, I've been counting my days differently. Billy Crystal put it so well in his memoir: "Having a grandchild does start another clock ticking. It's the how-old-will-I-be-when-they're-ten-and-then-fifteen-and-twenty-one-and-when-they're-married clock." Then he adds, "I couldn't help winding it up but I don't advise that you do. The numbers get very scary."[153]

Yes, the numbers do get very, very scary when I start figuring out how old I will be when my youngest grandson becomes a bar mitzvah. Will I make it to see my gorgeous grandchildren walk down the aisle at their weddings? I am crushed by the thought that I won't always be there with my family, that there will be great milestones in their lives that I will miss out on. When that time comes, how will they remember me? Don't take this the wrong way, but after all is said and done, they are the only ones who will remember me. That's life! Just ask Mr. Sears.

Sears, Roebuck, and Company, founded in 1893, came to symbolize the American way of life. By the mid-1950s, one in every five Americans shopped at Sears. As a symbol of its success, the company built the Sears Tower in Chicago. At the time it was built, this 1,450-foot skyscraper was the tallest of its kind. The head of the company explained, "We are the largest company in the country, and so it is fitting that we should have the largest headquarters in the country." But times changed, and time moved on ... and now the Sears Tower is the Willis Tower. That's life!

It was Charles de Gaulle who said, "Cemeteries are filled with irreplaceable people."[154] But the fact is we are all replaceable, to everyone except our family! I'm a husband, a father, a grandfather, a brother ... no one else will be able to fill those roles.

Now I'm going to fill all the time I have on my hands by

making memories for my family. Money, they can make for themselves. Only I can leave them memories! I thought of this when I read of a rabbinic colleague describing how he had met with the family of a member who had passed away to prepare his eulogy.

"Tell me about your father," the rabbi asked.

After a long silence, one of his sons volunteered, "Dad loved golf."

The rabbi responded that that was nice, but "What else did he love? What were his passions?"

Golf, they all agreed ... just golf.

"Just golf? What did he dream of? What were his values, his causes?"

"Well, he always wanted to live on a golf course."

And so the rabbi wrote, "I prepared a eulogy all about golf. It's not so hard to do: eighteen is the numeric value for the Hebrew word *chai*, which means life."

We can all do better than that. That's how I intend to live the coming years with my family—doing a lot better than that—so that someday, in fifty years, when my great-great-granddaughter Michelle Wohlberg has to fill out her bat mitzvah questionnaire and has to write something about the person after whom she is named, she will be told something really nice about me. I am spending the rest of my life making sure she feels good about her name and the person after whom she was named. I was not fortunate enough to have meaningful memories of my grandparents. I thank God every day for making it possible for me to create memories for my grandchildren.

W. Somerset Maugham once wrote, "What makes old age hard to bear is not the failing of one's faculties, mental and physical, but the burden of one's memories."[155] I don't see it that way. My memories are not a burden! In fact, I want to create a lot more of them!

Remember the words of William Faulkner: "The past is never dead. It's not even past."[156]

CONCLUSION

It's never too late ... it's later than you think.

—Mitchell Wohlberg

I 'm not going to say that I saved the best for last, but I will tell you that of the over two thousand sermons I have delivered to my congregation, the one I delivered in 1994 on the occasion of my fiftieth birthday proved for many to be the most memorable. It was entitled "It's Never Too Late ... It's Later Than You Think." When the sermon was over, everyone present was given a business-size card. On one side was written "It's Never Too Late." The other side read "It's Later Than You Think." To this day, there are people who show me that they still carry that card in their wallet.

There was something about the dichotomy and seeming contradiction of the phrases that struck a chord. I was later to learn that these two phrases are also found engraved in a fifteenth-century tunnel in Oxford. I first started thinking of them on Sunday, December 13, 1992. On that day, I was being honored by the Zionist Organization of America. Me ... and Larry King. My speech, if I must say so myself, was really good! So much so that when King got up to speak, his opening words were "If I die, get Wohlberg to do the funeral."

I'll never forget how those words struck me—and on so many different levels. It was a compliment, of course, but it was also as a puzzle. "If I die?" Larry, darling, it's *when*, no *if*s, *and*s, or *but*s about it ... as Larry King learned on January 23, 2021.

There's some of Larry King in so many of us. Some of us are forever putting off buying a plot or securing life insurance or going for an annual physical. As if it will all go away if we just ignore it. You can try to live that way if you want to, but you will only be kidding yourself!

Just ask a woman named Jacqueline Kennedy Onassis. Shortly before she died, she said to a friend about her cancer, "I don't get it. I did everything right to take care of myself, and look what happened. Why in the world did I do all those push-ups?" You can be Jackie Kennedy. You can be in the best of shape and well taken care of. That won't change the fact that the clock is always ticking, and you can never be sure when it will stop. Always remember: it's later than you think!

But that's only half the story!

Strangely enough, while our physical energy diminishes, our insight and wisdom seem to increase. As we get older, we realize that many of our childhood dreams would not have made us happy. We discover a painful truth that purpose and meaning in life are not defined by the size of our house or by the make of the car we drive or by the number of shoes we have. Other things become important—meaningful things. And that's the beauty of life. It's never too late.

It's never too late to learn, to be, to reach out, to love, to grow. Right after the birth of one of my sons, I rushed away to do a funeral. While my children were growing up, I'm sorry to say, I often gave priority to my rabbinic roles. But fortunately, they—and I—discovered there is always time to learn. Once, when my sons were in their twenties, they asked if I would like to go to Philadelphia one night for a concert. I looked at my calendar—it was June, the busiest time of the year, and I had a full day's schedule. But that didn't matter. Off I went to Philadelphia to see Pink Floyd.

It was quite a night. There we were, lined up with a huge crowd outside of Veterans Stadium, and one son turned to me and said, "Dad, I think you're going to be the only rabbi here tonight!" But that was all right. I was with my kids!

Inside the stadium, a more shocking realization hit me. I looked around at the sold-out crowd. Seventy thousand people, and I was the oldest man in the place. Oh, how depressing. Until the show started. The band came out, and I realized they were older than me. (Did I enjoy the concert? Well, two weeks later, I went with my boys to New York to see them again.)

That scene took place all across America that summer. Pink Floyd, the Rolling Stones, the Eagles, Billy Joel, and Elton John were all touring: it was referred to as *Geezer Rock*. Yes, it's never too late to teach an old dog new tricks. Sure, we have to surrender to life's decrees when they are inevitable. But perhaps they become inevitable only after we surrender to them. Sure, we have to accept the verdict of fate once it has come, but until then, why can't we fight as long as we can and as well as we can?

That is the spirit in which we ought to live. It's never too late. Some years ago, newspapers were filled with the story of Playmate of the Year Anna Nicole Smith marrying a Houston tycoon, eighty-nine-year-old billionaire J. Howard Marshall II. Newspapers reported that the twenty-six-year-old bride wore a low-cut satin gown while the groom was in a wheelchair. Commentators pointed out that this proved how where there's a will, there's a way. But I don't know if that's fair to either of the people involved.

I always think back to an ad I once saw in a Jewish newspaper: "Retired rabbi, aged seventy-nine. [If he's admitting to seventy-nine, then he must be at least seventy-nine.] Five foot seven. [I'm not sure what that has to do with anything, but that's what he says.] Seeks lady. [It doesn't say what he is seeking this lady for. Is it to be a companion? Or a wife? Or a friend? Or a housekeeper? Or a nurse? It doesn't say. It just says 'seeks lady.']"

And then he lists the qualifications that whoever answers this ad must have. "Must own own home. Must be financially independent. Must be attractive." And he goes on to specify what he means by *attractive*. "Must be between 5'2" and 5'4". Must weigh less than 135 pounds and must be no more than sixty-five years old." And then the ad says, "Telephone number (818) 342-3459, and you may call collect." And then comes my favorite line in the ad: "No calls after 8:00 P.M." That could mean one of two things: either he goes to sleep early or perhaps he goes out every night. My guess? At seventy-nine? If he's still advertising in the personals, then this is the kind of man who is going out every night, a man who is going to go down fighting! Yes, it's never too late.

I'm growing old. It's later than you think. But I'm also growing up, and it's never too late for that. I am a husband, a father, a grandfather, a brother ... but there is still a little boy in me. Every day, I try to be young enough to feel that it is never too late and to be old enough to know that it is later than I think.

M. Scott Peck has been immortalized by the three first words in his bestselling book *The Road Less Traveled*. These three words are remembered because they are so true, and the three words are "Life is tough!"

Life might be tough, but that's okay. It's also exciting and challenging and meaningful and can be beautiful if we work at it each and every day of our lives.

Thank you, God, for the lives of those who preceded me, for the lives of those who will follow me, and thank you, God, for my life as well.

Remember what Andy Rooney said: "I've learned that life is like a roll of toilet paper. The closer it gets to the end, the faster it goes."[157]

NOTES

1. Geoffrey Macnab, "Bill Murray: 'I know how to be sour,'" *Guardian*, December 31, 2003, https://www.theguardian.com/film/2004/jan/01/1.
2. Frank Rich, "Addicted to O.J.," *New York Times*, June 23, 1994, https://timesmachine.nytimes.com/timesmachine/1994/06/23/477877.html.
3. Jonathan Franklin, "He Came from Above," *Guardian*, November 11, 2008, https://www.theguardian.com/football/2008/nov/12/diego-maradona-argentina.
4. Maeve McDermott, "Taylor Swift inspired 65,000 people to register to vote, says Vote.org," *USA TODAY*, October 9, 2018, https://www.usatoday.com/story/life/music/2018/10/09/taylor-swift-inspired-65-000-people-register-vote-says-vote-org-tennessee-phil-bredesen-trump/1574916002/.
5. Peter Carlson, "Carlson's 10 Rules of Celebrity," *Washington Post*, December 5, 1993, https://www.washingtonpost.com/archive/lifestyle/magazine/1993/12/05/carlsons-10-laws-of-celebrity/0faa9361-f0b3-4319-9c5e-02e55304ac2b/.
6. Henry David Thoreau, *Civil Disobedience and Other Essays*, Dover thrift ed. (1849; repr., Mineola: Dover Publications).
7. Joseph Epstein, "Opinion: Is There a Doctor in the White House? Not if You Need an M.D.," *Wall Street Journal*, December 11, 2020, https://www.wsj.com/articles/is-there-a-

doctor-in-the-white-house-not-if-you-need-an-m-d-11607727380.

8. Heidi Stevens, "Column: We didn't just hate the Dr. Jill Biden op-ed by Joseph Epstein for its condescension. We hated it for its contempt for educators," *Chicago Tribune*, December 14, 2020, https://www.chicagotribune.com/columns/heidi-stevens/ct-heidi-stevens-wsj-dr-biden-anti-teacher-rant-1214-20201214-7dognuov7bdt5d5q4ts2lwc65q-story.html.

9. Greg Kandra, "Desperate for a Paris Hilton Fix? Here," *CBS News*, June 18, 2007, https://www.cbsnews.com/news/desperate-for-a-paris-hilton-fix-here/.

10. We assume the joke is that "dumb jock" Joe Theismann misremembered the name of *Albert* Einstein, but the real story might be rather more beautiful and interesting. Apparently, a very smart guy named Norman Einstein was a high school friend of Joe Theismann. Read more here: https://jimcofer.com/2009/10/29/righting-the-wrongs-joe-theismann/.

11. Bill Carter, "The Media Business; NBC Asks Leno to Work Late Through End of the Decade," March 30, 2004, https://www.nytimes.com/2004/03/30/business/the-media-business-nbc-asks-leno-to-work-late-through-end-of-the-decade.html.

12. As this interesting letter to the *New York Times* explains in detail, this entire exchange is apocryphal, and while a version of it did occur in real life (with Hemingway as the one put in his place and critic Mary Colum providing the quick retort), it was only later that Hemingway recycled the incident into a story and replaced himself with Fitzgerald. "The Rich Are Different," Letters, *New York Times*, November 13, 1988, https://www.nytimes.com/1988/11/13/books/l-the-rich-are-different-907188.html.

13. "Lance Armstrong's statement of August 23, 2012," *Los*

Angeles Times, August 23, 2012, https://www.latimes.com/sports/la-xpm-2012-aug-23-la-lance-armstrongs-statement-of-august-23-2012-20120823-story.html.

14. Laura M. Holson, "Nothing Left to Buy? Pondering the Indiscreet Charm of the Superrich," *New York Times*, March 2, 2000, https://www.nytimes.com/2000/03/03/business/nothing-left-to-buy-pondering-the-indiscreet-charm-of-the-superrich.html.

15. Jeff Bezos, "Letter to Shareholders," 1998, http://media.corporate-ir.net/media_files/irol/97/97664/reports/Shareholderletter98.pdf.

16. Despite the popular attribution, Einstein said no such thing, and the statement is first recorded in an article about a twelve-step program. See more here: https://quoteinvestigator.com/2017/03/23/same/ https://quoteinvestigator.com/2017/03/23/same/.

17. Frida Ghitis, "Are Men Stupid?" *CNN*, April 23, 2012, https://www.cnn.com/2012/04/23/opinion/ghitis-men-stupid/index.html.

18. David S. Broder, "The Democrats and the Mule Rule," *Washington Post*, November 11, 2004, https://www.washingtonpost.com/archive/opinions/2004/11/07/the-democrats-and-the-mule-rule/c0c15cb3-bcb7-4786-81d6-f0f9bd2f5d41/. This proverb-like wisdom has also been attributed to L. Mendel Rivers, or it might be, as Mitch McConnell claims, simply an old Kentucky saying.

19. As quoted in Mark A. Barondess, *What Were You Thinking? $600-per-Hour Legal Advice on Relationships, Marriage & Divorce* (Beverly Hills: Phoenix Books, 2005).

20. Al Franken, *Oh, the Things I Know! A Guide to Success, or, Failing That, Happiness* (New York: Dutton Adult, 2002), 9.

21. David Brooks, "American is Having a Moral Convulsion," *The Atlantic*, October 5, 2020, https://www.theatlantic.com/ideas/archive/2020/10/collapsing-levels-trust-are-devastating-america/616581/.

22. Wikipedia, s.v. "Hedgehog's dilemma," last modified June 15, 2021, 4:07, https://en.wikipedia.org/wiki/Hedgehog%27s_dilemma#cite_note-2.

23. William Clinton, "The President's News Conference with President Nelson Mandela of South Africa in Cape Town," *Public Papers of the Presidents of the United States* (US Government Publishing Office, March 27, 1998), 448. https://www.govinfo.gov/content/pkg/PPP-1998-book1/html/PPP-1998-book1-doc-pg448.htm.

24. Anna Brown, "Most Democrats who are looking for a relationship would not consider dating a Trump voter," Pew Research Center, April 4, 2020, https://www.pewresearch.org/fact-tank/2020/04/24/most-democrats-who-are-looking-for-a-relationship-would-not-consider-dating-a-trump-voter/.

25. Jennifer Wright, "If You Are Married to a Trump Supporter, Divorce Them," *Harper's Bazaar*, August 11, 2017, https://www.harpersbazaar.com/culture/politics/a11664976/divorce-trump-supporters/.

26. Jonah Goldberg, "Outrage Overload," *The Dispatch*, April 28, 2021, https://gfile.thedispatch.com/p/tucker-carlson-tim-scott-policing-reform.

27. Andrew Sullivan, "If We Want to End the Border Crisis, It's Time to Give Trump His Wall," *New York Magazine*, June 22, 2018, https://nymag.com/intelligencer/2018/06/to-end-the-border-crisis-for-good-give-trump-his-wall.html.

28. He might have said it (or something very similar). However,

so have several other people, it seems. Read more here: https://www.barrypopik.com/index.php/new_york_city/entry/everyone_is_entitled_to_his_own_opinion_but_not_his_own_facts.

29. Gus Lubin, "This Army Exercise Was So Useless It Inspired A Psychological Theory," *Business Insider*, December 26, 2012, https://www.businessinsider.com/israeli-army-inspired-illusion-of-validity-2012-12.

30. Wikipedia, s.v. "Samuel Goldwyn," last modified June 29, 2021, 19:24, https://en.wikipedia.org/wiki/Samuel_Goldwyn#Goldwynisms.

31. Mary Korzan, *When You Thought I Wasn't Looking: A Book of Thanks for Mom* (Kansas City: Andrews McMeel Publishing, 2004). Formatting for the poem taken from the author's website: https://www.whenyouthoughtiwasntlooking.com.

32. Monica Langley, "Italian Firm Fashions a New Look Tailor-Made for Indulgent Parents," *Wall Street Journal*, August 24, 2000, https://www.wsj.com/articles/SB96707041912721052.

33. Benjamin Blech, *Taking Stock: A Spiritual Guide to Rising Above Life's Financial Ups and Downs* (New York: Amacom, 2003) 59.

34. Tom Toles, "Opinion: He who dies with the most toys now loses!" *Washington Post*, October 24, 2016, https://www.washingtonpost.com/news/opinions/wp/2016/10/24/he-who-dies-with-the-most-toys-now-loses/.

35. Ruby Deevoy, "Why Decluttering Is Good for Your mental Health," *Calm Moment*, January 4, 2021. https://www.calmmoment.com/living/why-decluttering-is-good-for-your-mental-health/.

36. John Pielmeier, *Agnes of God: A Drama* (New York; Samuel French, 1982).

37. Danielle Braff, "Plastic surgeons say business is up, partly because clients don't like how they look on Zoom," *Washington Post*, December 7, 2020, https://www.washingtonpost.com/road-to-recovery/plastic-surgery-cosmetic-covid-zoom/2020/12/07/6283e6d2-35a2-11eb-b59c-adb7153d10c2_story.html.

38. Cathy Alter, "'My Beautiful Mommy': How a Picture Book Explains Liposuction to Kids," *The Atlantic*, March 26, 2011, https://www.theatlantic.com/entertainment/archive/2011/03/my-beautiful-mommy-how-a-picture-book-explains-liposuction-to-kids/73051/.

39. Mary Duenwald, "How Young Is Too Young to Have a Nose Job and Breast Implants?" *New York Times*, September 28, 2004, https://www.nytimes.com/2004/09/28/health/how-young-is-too-young-to-have-a-nose-job-and-breast-implants.html.

40. This is not the same article, but it makes the same point. Marlene Schwartz, "Some People Would Give Life or Limb Not to be Fat," *Yale News*, May 16, 2006, https://news.yale.edu/2006/05/16/some-people-would-give-life-or-limb-not-be-fat.

41. "Being beautiful isn't Easy, Halle Berry says," *Deseret News*, August 3, 2004, https://www.deseret.com/2004/8/3/19843269/being-beautiful-isn-t-easy-halle-berry-says.

42. Judd Yadid, "Israel's Iron Lady Unfiltered: 17 Golda Meir Quotes on Her 117th Birthday," *Haaretz*, April 10, 2018, https://www.haaretz.com/.premium-17-golda-meir-quotes-on-her-117th-birthday-1.5356683.

43. Mariel Reed, "'The most courageous act is still to think for yourself. Aloud' 25 Coco Chanel quotes to live by," *Marie Claire*, October 4, 2016, https://www.marieclaire.co.uk/fashion/coco-chanel-s-25-snappiest-quotes-54026.

44. This is another saying that has been attributed to many different people (including Dorothy Parker), but the origin

likely goes back to the early nineteenth century (and possibly even before that). For more information, see this link: https://quoteinvestigator.com/2020/09/25/skin-deep/.

45. Enid Nemy, "Leona Helmsley, Hotel Queen, Dies at 87," *New York Times*, August 20, 2007, https://www.nytimes.com/2007/08/20/nyregion/20cnd-helmsley.html.

46. He possibly did say it, but it's also a popular trope, and it appears in *Grease* among other films and shows.

47. For the full text of the poem, please see this link: https://poets.org/poem/village-blacksmith.

48. "Tiger Woods' apology: Full transcript," *CNN*, February 19, 2010, http://www.cnn.com/2010/US/02/19/tiger.woods.transcript/index.html.

49. Mike Michalowicz, "Your Business Can't Love You Back: What Sam Walton Taught me about Life," *Octane Magazine*, September 2012, https://www.eonetwork.org/octane-magazine/september-2012/you-business-cant-love-you-back.

50. Warren Hoge, "Diplomats at U.N. Surprised by Danforth's Resignation," *New York Times*, December 3, 2004, https://www.nytimes.com/2004/12/03/world/diplomats-at-un-surprised-by-danforths-resignation.html.

51. Associated Press, "Sentence Imposed on Surgeon General's Son," *New York Times*, August 30, 1994, https://www.nytimes.com/1994/08/30/us/sentence-imposed-on-surgeon-general-s-son.html.

52. Sam Howe Verhovek, "Pro Football; At Issue: Hold a Baby or Hold That Line?" *New York Times*, October 20, 1993, https://www.nytimes.com/1993/10/20/us/pro-football-at-issue-hold-a-baby-or-hold-that-line.html.

53. Alice Schroeder, *The Snowball: Warren Buffett and the Business of Life* (New York: Bantam Books, 2008).

54. Here is the full text of her commencement address: https://www.wellesley.edu/events/commencement/archives/1990 commencement/commencementaddress.

55. Katherine Rosman, "Lady of the Lakers," *New York Times*, January 2, 2021, https://www.nytimes.com/2021/01/02/style/jeanie-buss-lakers.html.

56. Jacon Furedi, "Marilyn Monroe: Defining quotes from a cultural icon on what would have been her 90th birthday," *The Independent*, June 1, 2016, https://www.independent.co.uk/news/people/marilyn-monroe-defining-quotes-what-would-have-been-her-90th-birthday-a7059611.html.

57. Dean LaBerge, "World Compliment Day," *Grizzly Gazette*, February 23, 2021, https://thegrizzlygazette.com/albertas-business2/world-compliment-day/.

58. Bob Greene, "Opinion: I Actually Thanked a Teacher," *Wall Street Journal*, April 12, 2017, https://www.wsj.com/articles/i-actually-thanked-a-teacher-1492037505.

59. Ross Johnson, "James Caan: What I've Learned," *Esquire*, January 29, 2007, https://www.esquire.com/entertainment/a799/esq0903-sep-wil/.

60. Vinson Cunningham, "How Are Audiences Adapting to the Age of Virtual Theatre," *New Yorker*, October 5, 2020, https://www.newyorker.com/magazine/2020/10/12/how-are-audiences-adapting-to-the-age-of-virtual-theatre.

61. Lauraine Farr, "Groupthink," Islip Library, June 22, 2018, https://www.isliplibrary.org/groupthink/.

62. William L. Shirer, *The Nightmare Years, 1930–1940* (New York: Little, Brown and Company, 1984).

63. Michael C. Bender, "'It's Kind of Like an Addiction': On the Road With Trump's Rally Diehards," *Wall Street Journal*, September 6, 2019, https://www.wsj.com/articles/

its-kind-of-like-an-addiction-on-the-road-with-trumps-rally-diehards-11567762200.

64. The full text of that essay is quite short and (for those who are curious) available here: https://oregonstate.edu/instruct/phl201/modules/Philosophers/Kierkegaard/kierkegaard_the_crowd_is_untruth.html.

65. Like so many quotes attributed to Einstein, this one is also unlikely to be his. For more information, see this article: https://quoteinvestigator.com/2012/10/18/follows-crowd/.

66. Robert Cialdini, *Influence: The Psychology of Persuasion* (New York: Harper Business, 2006).

67. This was something she shared in a 1997 interview, a clip of which can be found here: https://www.facebook.com/watch/?v=709174696359554.

68. Carl Bernstein, *A Woman in Charge: The Life of Hillary Rodham Clinton* (New York: Knopf, 2007).

69. For the full text of the poem, please see this link: http://www.robertburns.org/works/97.shtml.

70. Judith Viorst, *Grown-Up Marriage: What We Know, Wish We Had Known, and Still Need to Know About Being Married* (New York: Simon and Schuster, 2008).

71. Rabbi Perry Netter, *Divorce Is a Mitzvah: A Practical Guide to Finding Wholeness and Holiness When Your Marriage Dies* (Woodstock: Jewish Lights Publishing, 2002), 21.

72. Mitch Albom, *Tuesdays with Morrie: An Old Man, a Young Man, and Life's Greatest Lesson* (New York: Doubleday, 1997).

73. Dave Itzkoff, "Chris Rock Tried to Warn Us," *New York Times*, September 16, 2020, https://www.nytimes.com/2020/09/16/arts/television/chris-rock-fargo.html.

74. Rebecca Ford, "Kim Kardashian Divorcing Kris Humphries After 72 Days of Marriage," *Hollywood Reporter*, October 31, 2011,

https://www.hollywoodreporter.com/news/general-news/
kim-kardashian-divorce-kris-humphries-255249/.

75. Cara Buckley, "How a Town House in N.Y. Went From
Dream to Nightmare," *New York Times*, July 11, 2006, https://
www.nytimes.com/2006/07/11/nyregion/11doctor.html.

76. Eun Kyung Kim, "Dad surprises stepdad at daughter's
wedding—with both walking bride down aisle," Today
(website), September 29, 2015, https://www.today.com/
parents/dad-surprises-stepdad-daughters-wedding-both-
walking-bride-down-aisle-t46981.

77. Celebretainment, "Gwyneth Paltrow takes 'positives' from
divorce," AP News, June 1, 2017, https://apnews.com/article/
18a9ab839a374c78af47524b227fe76a.

78. Edward Dolnick, "Why Do Women Outlive Men?" *Washington
Post*, August 13, 1991, https://www.washingtonpost.com/archive/
lifestyle/wellness/1991/08/13/why-do-women-outlive-men/
ec631b85-a225-4ade-aea3-b2678356005f/.

79. George Carlin, *When Will Jesus Bring the Pork Chops?* (New
York: Hyperion, 2005).

80. Demetri Martin, *This Is a Book* (New York: Grand Central
Publishing, 2011).

81. Julia Prodis Sulek, "After 6 Months of Lockdown, What Do
You Miss the Most?" *Mercury News*, September 12, 2020,
https://www.mercurynews.com/2020/09/12/after-6-months-
of-covid-19-lockdown-what-do-you-miss-the-most/.

82. Tim Stickings, "Inside an inflatable 'room of hugs' where
Italian care home residents can touch their loved ones
through plastic screens," *Daily Mail*, January 3, 2021, https://
www.dailymail.co.uk/news/article-9107601/Italian-care-
home-residents-visitors-room-hugs.html.

83. "Hugging Is Healthy," Information Technology Services,

Caltech, accessed June 30, 2021, http://www.its.caltech.edu/~rem/healthy.html.

84. D. T. Max, "Annals of Medicine: Paging Dr. Robot," *New Yorker*, September 30, 2019, https://www.newyorker.com/magazine/2019/09/30/paging-dr-robot.

85. Eli Saslow, "Strug's Golden Years Come After Olympics," *Washington Post*, August 9, 2004, https://www.washingtonpost.com/wp-dyn/articles/A52856-2004Aug9.html.

86. Maggie Parker, "The 'irrational desire' driving millennials and Gen Z into depression," *Yahoo Life*, January 3, 2018, https://www.yahoo.com/lifestyle/irrational-desire-driving-millennials-gen-z-depression-222357005.html.

87. Maureen Dowd, "An Ideal Husband," *New York Times*, July 6 2008, https://www.nytimes.com/2008/07/06/opinion/06dowd.html.

88. "To Trust and Cherish: Rules to Love By," Letters to the Editor, *New York Times*, July 9, 2008, https://www.nytimes.com/2008/07/09/opinion/l09dowd.html.

89. Bernard Berkowitz, Mildred Newman, and Jean Owen, *How to Be Your Own Best Friend* (New York: Ballantine Books, 2016).

90. Tim Russert, *Big Russ & Me: Father & Son; Lessons of Life* (New York: Miramax Publishing, 2004).

91. Garrison Keillor, *Leaving Home* (New York: Penguin Books, 1990).

92. Peter Beinart, "How Could Modern Orthodox Judaism Produce Jared Kushner?" *Forward*, January 31, 2017, https://forward.com/opinion/361826/how-could-modern-orthodox-judaism-produce-jared-kushner/.

93. Shane Harris, Carol D. Leonnig, Greg Jaffe, and Josh Dawsey, "Kushner's overseas contacts raise concerns as foreign

officials seek leverage," *Washington Post*, February 27, 2018, https://www.washingtonpost.com/world/national-security/kushners-overseas-contacts-raise-concerns-as-foreign-officials-seek-leverage/2018/02/27/16bbc052-18c3-11e8-942d-16a950029788_story.html.

94. "Jared Kushner Appears to Be in Trouble," *Economist*, March 8, 2018, https://www.economist.com/united-states/2018/03/08/jared-kushner-appears-to-be-in-trouble.

95. Jennifer Medina, Katie Benner, and Kate Taylor, "Actresses, Business Leaders and Other Wealthy Parents Charged in U.S. College Entry Fraud," *New York Times*, March 12, 2019, https://www.nytimes.com/2019/03/12/us/college-admissions-cheating-scandal.html.

96. Brian Costa, "At USC, Admissions Cheating Scandal Runs Deeper," *Wall Street Journal*, March 13, 2019, https://www.wsj.com/articles/at-usc-admissions-cheating-scandal-runs-deeper-11552505533.

97. Jennifer Senior, *All Joy and No Fun: The Paradox of Modern Parenthood* (New York: Ecco Press, 2014).

98. David Brooks, "The Great Seduction," *New York Times*, June 10, 2008, https://www.nytimes.com/2008/06/10/opinion/10iht-edbrooks.1.13606389.html.

99. Here is the full text of the commencement address given at Lewis & Clark College on May 10, 2014: https://college.lclark.edu/live/files/17133-edelman-commencement-speech lewis--clark.

100. T. M. Shine, *Fathers Aren't Supposed to Die: Five Brothers Reunite to Say Good-Bye* (New York: Simon and Schuster, 2000).

101. Dylan Thomas, *A Child's Christmas in Wales* (New York: New Directions, 1995).

102. Dan Elliot, "Thompson Wanted One Final Blast," *Spokesman-*

Review, February 24, 2005, https://www.spokesman.com/stories/2005/feb/24/thompson-wanted-one-final-blast/.

103. Ezekiel J. Emanuel, "Why I Hope to Die at 75," *Atlantic*, October 2014, https://www.theatlantic.com/magazine/archive/2014/10/why-i-hope-to-die-at-75/379329/.

104. For the full text of the poem, please see this link: https://poets.org/poem/do-not-go-gentle-good-night.

105. Philip Roth, *Everyman* (New York: Houghton Mifflin Harcourt, 2006).

106. Kiley Armstrong, "Forbes: 'While Alive, He Lived," AP News, February 26, 1990, https://apnews.com/article/62b34 19879a9e509b08ccc4619dee014

107. George Tucker, "Feisty and Outspoken, Miss Lillian Left Vivid Impressions," *Virginian Pilot*, August 11, 1997, https://scholar.lib.vt.edu/VA-news/VA-Pilot/issues/1997/vp970811/08080798.htm.

108. Isaac Metzker, *A Bintel Brief: Sixty Years of Letters from the Lower East Side to the Jewish Daily Forward* (New York: Schocken Books, 1990).

109. Brooks Atkinson, *Once Around the Sun* (New York: Harcourt, Brace, & Company, 1951).

110. Dennis Prager, *Happiness Is a Serious Problem: A Human Nature Repair Manual* (New York: William Morrow Paperbacks, 1998).

111. Mike Sager, "Kirk Douglas: What I've Learned," *Esquire*, January 29, 2007, https://www.esquire.com/entertainment/interviews/a1585/learned-kirk-douglas-0401/.

112. The Dalai Lama and Arthur C. Brooks, "Opinion: Dalai Lama; Behind Our Anxiety, the Fear of Being Unneeded," *New York Times*, November 4, 2016, https://www.nytimes.com/2016/11/04/opinion/dalai-lama-behind-our-anxiety-the-fear-of-being-unneeded.html.

113. Dean Ornish, *Love & Survival: The Scientific Basis for the Healing Power of Intimacy* (New York: Harper, 1998).

114. George Vecsey, "Indomitable Russell Values One Accolade Above the Rest," *New York Times*, February 12, 2011, https://www.nytimes.com/2011/02/13/sports/basketball/13russell.html.

115. Dr. Ron Jones, "Warren Buffet on Unconditional Love," *Something Good*, July 10, 2010, https://www.somethinggoodradio.org/blog/warren-buffett-on-unconditional-love-2/.

116. Associated Press, "1970s 'Bear' Bryant commercial resurfaces each Mother's Day," *Arkansas Democrat Gazette*, May 9, 2021, https://www.al.com/alabamafootball/2013/05/on_mothers_day_a_look_back_at.html.

117. Margaret Atwood, *The Handmaid's Tale* (New York: Knopf Doubleday Publishing Group, 1985).

118. Glenn Kessler, Salvador Rizzo, and Meg Kelly. "Trump's false or misleading claims total 30,573 over 4 years," *Washington Post*, January 23, 2021, https://www.washingtonpost.com/politics/2021/01/24/trumps-false-or-misleading-claims-total-30573-over-four-years/.

119. NBC News, "Conway: Press Secretary Gave 'Alternative Facts,'" *Meet the Press*, January 22, 2017, https://www.nbcnews.com/meet-the-press/video/conway-press-secretary-gave-alternative-facts-860142147643.

120. David Greenberg, "Are Clinton and Trump the Biggest Liars Ever to Run for President?" *Politico*, July/August 2016, https://www.politico.com/magazine/story/2016/07/2016-donald-trump-hillary-clinton-us-history-presidents-liars-dishonest-fabulists-214024/.

121. Walter Scott, *Marmion: A Tale of Flodden Field in Six Cantos* (self-pub., CreateSpace, 2017).

122. Erich Fromm, *The Sane Society* (New York: Rinehart, 1955).

123. For the full text of Khalil Gibran's poem, please see this link: https://poets.org/poem/children-1.

124. Judith Viorst, *Necessary Losses: The Loves, Illusions, Dependencies, and Impossible Expectations That All of Us Have to Give Up in Order to Grow* (New York: Simon and Schuster, 1998).

125. Mitch Albom, *Tuesdays with Morrie: An Old Man, a Young Man, and Life's Greatest Lesson* (New York: Doubleday, 1997).

126. Associated Press, "Hirschbeck's son brings umpire, Alomar together," ESPN, May 15, 2000, http://www.espn.com/mlb/news/2000/0515/533467.html.

127. Thomas de Quincy, "The Last Days of Emanuel Kant," Berfrois, March 15, 2013 (first published in 1827), https://www.berfrois.com/2013/03/last-days-immanuel-kant-thomas-de-quincey/.

128. This saying is attributed to many people and has clearly evolved over time. Read more here: https://quoteinvestigator.com/2017/08/19/resentment/.

129. William Safire, "On Language: It Is What it Is," *New York Times*, May 3, 2006, https://www.nytimes.com/2006/03/05/magazine/it-is-what-it-is.html.

130. Hannah Beech, Alissa J. Rubin, Anatoly Kurmanaev, and Ruth Maclean, "The Covid-19 Riddle: Why Does the Virus Wallop Some Places and Spare Others?" *New York Times*, May 3, 2020, updated September 25. 2020, https://www.nytimes.com/2020/05/03/world/asia/coronavirus-spread-where-why.html.

131. Kate Bower, *Everything Happens for a Reason: And Other Lies I've Loved* (New York: Random House, 2018).

132. "Ethics of the Fathers: Chapter One," Chabad, accessed June 30, 2021, https://www.chabad.org/library/article_cdo/aid/2165/jewish/Chapter-One.htm#v3.

133. David Von Drehle, "One Page at a Time," *Washington Post*, May 3, 2004, https://www.washingtonpost.com/archive/lifestyle/2004/05/03/one-page-at-a-time/a44af9b9-a922-4c35-bfc1-a9d9fd1674f4/.

134. Diane Curtis, "Advice from one who failed bar exam 47 times: Try again, again and again," *California Bar Journal* (February 2004), http://archive.calbar.ca.gov/archive/Archive.aspx?articleId=54802&categoryId=54503&month=2&year=2004.

135. The full text of her commencement address can be found here: https://www.wellesley.edu/events/commencement/archives/1996commencement.

136. Anton LaGuardia, "NS Profile: The Israeli Settlements," *New Statesman*, May 26, 2003, https://www.newstatesman.com/node/157713.

137. Noah Lior, "What You See from Here," *Jerusalem Post*, January 21, 2016, https://www.jpost.com/magazine/what-you-see-from-here-442316.

138. Quoted in Dwight Garner, "Book Review: Inside the List," *New York Times*, October 17, 2004, https://www.nytimes.com/2004/10/17/books/review/inside-the-list.html.

139. Stephen Colbert, "I believe in this president," *Guardian*, May 1, 2006, https://www.theguardian.com/world/2006/may/02/usa.georgebush.

140. Michael Wex, *Born to Kvetch: Yiddish Language and Culture in All of Its Moods* (New York: St. Martin's Press, 2005).

141. Dale Carnegie, *How to Win Friends & Influence People* (New York: Simon and Schuster, 2009).

142. Dan Ellsworth, "Thou Shalt Not Whine," *Public Square*

Magazine, January 14. 2021, https://publicsquaremag.org/
faith/thou-shalt-not-whine/.

143. David Conrads, "One man's crusade to stop the world from
complaining," *Christian Science Monitor*, February 19, 2008,
https://www.csmonitor.com/USA/Society/2008/0219/
p20s01-ussc.html.

144. Lou Holtz, *Winning Every Day: A Game Plan for Success* (New
York: Harper Business, 1998).

145. Rebecca Fenton, "Laura Ingraham: Romney Has to Bring
'A' Game to Beat Obama," ABC News Radio, January 29,
2012, http://abcnewsradioonline.com/politics-news/laura-
ingraham-romney-has-to-bring-a-game-to-beat-obama.
html.

146. Gene Weingarten, "Fatal Distraction: Forgetting a Child
in the Backseat of a Car Is a Horrifying Mistake. Is It a
Crime?" *Washington Post*, March 8, 2009, https://www.
washingtonpost.com/lifestyle/magazine/fatal-distraction-
forgetting-a-child-in-thebackseat-of-a-car-is-a-horrifying-
mistake-is-it-a-crime/2014/06/16/8ae0fe3a-f580-11e3-a3a5-
42be35962a52_story.html.

147. Ilan Ben Zion, "Leave the Cannoli, Take the Baby," *Times
of Israel*, July 16, 2013, https://www.timesofisrael.com/
leave-the-cannoli-take-the-baby/.

148. Bruce Lee, "Becoming a Warrior," parts 1 and 2, Bruce
Lee (website), February 28, 2018 and July 3, 2018,
https://brucelee.com/podcast-blog/2018/2/28/87-becoming-
a-warrior; https://brucelee.com/podcast-blog/2018/7/3/105
-becoming-a-warrior.

149. Celestine Chua, *101 Things to Do Before You Die*, Personal
Excellence. Ebook available from https://personalexcellence.
co/blog/bucket-list/.

150. James Barron, "Taking a Bullet, Gaining a Cause: James S. Brady Dies at 73," *New York Times*, August 4, 2014, https://www.nytimes.com/2014/08/05/us/politics/james-s-brady-symbol-of-fight-for-gun-control-dies-at-73.html.

151. Michel de Montaigne, *The Essays: A Selection* (London: Penguin Classics, 1994).

152. Appropriately enough, his character said this in the 2007 movie *The Bucket List*.

153. Billy Crystal, *Still Foolin' 'Em: Where I've Been, Where I'm Going, and Where the Hell Are My Keys?* (New York: St. Martin's Griffin, 2013), 226.

154. Or maybe Georges Clemenceau or Winston Churchill said it. Or possibly it is an old Polish saying.

155. W. Somerset Maugham, *Point of View: Five Essays* (New York: Heinemann, 1958).

156. William Faulkner, *Requiem for a Nun* (New York: Harper Perennial Classis, 2013).

157. Probably not Andy Rooney, in fact, though no less true even if he didn't say it. See here for more information: https://www.snopes.com/fact-check/what-ive-learned/.

Made in the USA
Middletown, DE
19 September 2021